Josh Biilings

Josh Billings, hiz sayings:

with comic illustrations

Josh Billings

Josh Billings, hiz sayings:
with comic illustrations

ISBN/EAN: 9783337733674

Printed in Europe, USA, Canada, Australia, Japan

Cover: Foto ©ninafisch / pixelio.de

More available books at **www.hansebooks.com**

JOSH BILLINGS,

𝕳𝖎𝖟 𝕾𝖆𝖞𝖎𝖓𝖌𝖘.

WITH COMIC ILLUSTRATIONS.

NEW YORK:
CARLETON, PUBLISHER, 413 *BROADWAY*
M DCCC LXVII.

Tred litely, dear reader, for the ^way^ iz ruff. This book was got up tew sell, but if it don't prove tew be a sell, I shan't worry about it.

J. BILLINGS.

TO

DEAKON URIAH BILLINGS,

(A man ov menny virtues, and sum vices) this book iz completely dedikated — and may he hav the strength tew stand it.

Hiz own nephew,
JOSHUA BILLINGS.

CONTENTS.

		Page.
I.	JOSH BILLINGS ON THE MULE.	13
II.	JOSH BILLINGS INSURES HIS LIFE.	15
III.	REMARKS.	17
IV.	ANSWERS TO CORRESPONDENTS.	19
V.	A TABLOWS IN 4 ACKS.	22
VI.	FEMALE EDDIKASHUN.	25
VII.	DEPOZETIONS.	28
VIII.	WAR AND ARMY PHRAZES.	31
IX.	PASHUNCE OV JOB.	34
X.	FRIENDLY LETTER.	35
XI.	AFFURISIMS.	37
XII.	JOSH BILLINGS ON CATS.	40
XIII.	REMARKS.	43
XIV.	JOSH BILLINGS ADDRESSES THE BILLINGSVILLE SOWING SOSIETY.	45
XV.	NOSHUNS.	47
XVI.	SAYINS.	51
XVII.	REMARKS.	53
XVIII.	THE DEVIL'S PUTTY AND VARNISH.	56

CONTENTS.

		Page.
XIX.	MANIFEST DESTINY.	59
XX.	ANSWERS TO CONTRIBUTORS.	62
XXI.	ON DOGS.	64
XXII.	SAYINGS OF JOSH BILLINGS.	67
XXIII.	FASHION.	70
XXIV.	REMARKS.	73
XXV.	PROVERBIAL PIG.	75
XXVI.	PROVERBS.	77
XXVII.	ANSWERS TO CORRESPONDENTS.	79
XXVIII.	PROVERBS OF THE BILLINGS FAMILY.	82
XXIX.	A FU REMARKS.	85
XXX.	A LEKTURE TEW MALE YUNG MEN ONLY.	87
XXXI.	CLEVER FELLOWS.	90
XXXII.	AFFERISIMS	92
XXXIII.	ANSWERS TO CONTRIBUTORS.	94
XXXIV.	A SHORT AND VERY AFFEKTING ESSA ON MAN.	97
XXXV.	THE RASE KOARSE.	100
XXXVI.	"GIV THE DEVIL HIZ DUE."	106
XXXVII.	WATCH DOGS.	108
XXXVIII.	ANSWERS TO CONTRIBUTORS.	110
XXXIX.	REMARKS.	113
XL.	AN ESSA ONTO MUSIK.	117
XLI.	"MAN WAZ MADE TEW MOURN."	120
XLII.	PROVERBS.	122

CONTENTS.

xi

		Page
XLIII	KISSING CONSIDERED.	124
XLIV.	FOR A FU MINNITS AMONG THE SPEERITS.	128
XLV.	SAYINGS.	131
XLVI.	JOSH GOES TO LONG BRANCH.	133
XLVII.	TO MY LADY CORRESPONDENTS.	137
XLVIII.	ON WIDDERS.	140
XLIX.	THINGS THAT I DON'T HANKER AFTER TO SEE.	143
L.	ON COURTING.	145
LI.	REMARKS.	149
LII.	THE FAULT FINDER.	152
LIII.	PROVERBS.	154
LIV.	KOLIDING.	156
LV.	ON SNAIKS AND MUDTURKLES.	157
LVI.	TRUE BILLS.	161
LVII.	NARRATIF.	163
LVIII.	PHOTOGRAPHS.	167
LIX.	AFFERISIMS.	169
LX.	JOSH GITS ORFULLY BIT.	172
LXI.	THINGS THAT SUIT ME.	174
LXII.	MY FIRST GONG.	176
LXIII.	PROVERBS.	178
LXIV.	DISIPLIN IZ EVRATHING — IN 2 PARTS.	181
LXV.	CORRESPONDENTS.	183
LXVI.	JOSH BILLINGS AT SARATOGA SPRINGS.	186

CONTENTS.

		Page
LXVII.	NOT ENNY SHANGHI FOR ME.	189
LXVIII.	IS DISPOSING OF THINGS FOR CHARITABLE PURPOSES BI "LOT" A SIN.	191
LXIX.	ADVERTIZEMENT.	193
LXX.	OUT WEST.	196
LXXI.	SAYINS.	198
LXXII.	A WIMMIN'S LEAGUE MEETIN.	200
LXXIII.	A TRUE FISH STORY FOUNDED ON FAK.	203
LXXIV.	AT SARATOGA SPRINGS.	205
LXXV.	SPIRITUAL BELIEF OV THE BILLINGSES.	208
LXXVI.	JOSH BILLINGS CORRESPONDS WITH A "HAIR OIL AND VEGETABLE BITTERS MAN."	209
LXXVII.	PROVERBS.	213
LXXVIII.	DOMESTIK RECEIPTS IN FULL.	216
LXXIX.	FAKS.	218
LXXX.	ON LECTURES.	219
LXXXI.	YANKEE NOSHUNS.	222
LXXXII.	ATTENTION! SQUAD!	224
LXXXIII.	THE FUST BABY.	226
LXXXIV.	LAUGHING.	228
LXXXV.	PIONEERS.	229

JOSH BILLINGS.

I.

JOSH BILLINGS ON THE MULE.

The mule is haf hoss, and haf Jackass, and then kums tu a full stop, natur diskovering her mistake. Tha weigh more, akordin tu their heft, than enny other kreetur, except a crowbar. Tha kant hear enny quicker, nor further than the hoss, yet their ears are big enuff for snow shoes. You kan trust them with enny one whose life aint worth enny more than the mules. The only wa tu keep them into a paster, is tu turn them into a medder jineing, and let them jump out. Tha are reddy for use, just as soon as they will du tu abuse. Tha haint got enny friends, and will live on huckel berry brush, with an ockasional chanse at Kanada thissels. Tha are a modern invenshun, i dont think the Bible deludes tu them at tall. Tha sel for more money than enny other domestik animile. Yu kant tell their age by looking into their mouth, enny more than you kould a Mexican cannons.

Tha never hav no dissease that a good club wont heal. If tha ever die tha must kum rite tu life agin, for i never herd nobody sa " ded mule." Tha are like sum men, very korrupt at harte; ive known them tu be good mules for 6 months, just tu git a good chanse to kick sumbody. I never owned one, nor never mean to, unless there is a United Staits law passed, requiring it. The only reason why tha are pashunt, is bekause tha are ashamed ov themselfs. I have seen eddikated mules in a sirkus. Tha kould kick, and bite, tremenjis. I would not sa what I am forced tu sa again the mule, if his birth want an outrage, and man want tu blame for it. Enny man who is willing tu drive a mule, ought to be exempt by law from running for the legislatur. Tha are the strongest creeturs on earth, and heaviest, ackording tu their sise; I herd tell ov one who fell oph from the tow path, on the Eri kanawl, and sunk as soon as he touched bottom, but he kept rite on towing the boat tu the nex stashun, breathing thru his ears, which stuck out ov the water about 2 feet 6 inches; i did'nt see this did, but an auctioneer told me ov it, and i never knew an auctioneer tu lie unless it was absolutely convenient.

II.

JOSH BILLINGS INSURES HIS LIFE.

I kum to the conclusion, lately, that life waz so onsartin, that the only wa for me tu stand a fair chance with other folks, was to git my life insured, and so i kalled on the Agent of the "Garden Angel life insurance Co.," and answered the following questions, which waz put tu me over the top ov a pair of goold specks, by a slik little fat old feller, with a little round gray head, and az pretty a little belly on him az enny man ever owned: —

QUESTIONS.

1st—Are yu mail or femail? if so, Pleze state how long you have been so.

2d—Are yu subjec tu fits, and if so, do yu hav more than one at a time?

3d—What is yure precise fiteing weight?

4th—Did yu ever have enny ancestors, and if so, how much?

5th—What iz yure legal opinion ov the constitutionality ov the 10 commandments!

6th—Du yu ever hav enny nite mares?

7th—Are you married and single, or are yu a Bachelor?

8th — Do yu beleave in a futer state? if yu du, state it.

9th—What are yure private sentiments about a rush ov rats tu the head; can it be did successfully?

10th—Hav yu ever committed suiside. and if so, how did it seem to affect yu?

After answering the above questions, like a man in the confirmatif, the slik little fat old fellow with goold specks on, ced I was insured for life, and proberly would remain so for a term ov years. I thanked him, and smiled one ov my moste pensive smiles.

III.

REMARKS.

Tha tell me that them who hav the *harte diseaze* are liable tu di at enny time, but i hav known thousands tew reach a mean old age with it.

Fust appearances are ced tu be everything. I dont put all mi fathe into this saying; i think oysters and klams, for instanze, will bear looking into.

It strains a man's philosophee the wust kind tew laff when he gits beat.

Love aint one ov the vartues, bekauze it kant be controlled.

Wimmin are like flowers, a little dust ov squeezing makes them the more fragrant.

Charitee kant alwus be administered delikately. If you want to extrikate a crab from a dilemmer, yu hav got to take holt ov him just rite.

Men liv tu a *ripe* old age bi keeping *green*.

Dont hav enny more sekrets than yu kan keep yureself.

" Truth is mitey and will prevail; " so iz cider mitey, but yu hav got tew tap the barrell before it will prevale.

IV.

ANSWERS TO CORRESPONDENTS.

"*Amelia.*" — Yure inquiry, about the moste best time tu marry, dus yu grate credit, it iz a subject which i hav swet over a good deal, and i am real glad you spoke about it, mi spase wont allow me tu go into the thing, clean up to the hub, az i wud like tu, but in a few wurds, i will sa, i hav alwus considered cool weather, the moste best time.

"*Fred.*" — Yu aint obliged tu ask a gals mother, if yu ma go home with her from a partee, git the gals endorsement, and sale in; it iz proper enuff tu ask her tu take yure arm, but you haint got no rite tu put yure arm around her waste, unless yu meet a Bear on the rode, and then yu are bound tu take yure arm away, just az soon az the Bear gits safely by.

"*Whip.*" — Yu are rite. Mules live tu a long age, iv'e known them miself, tu live 100 years, and not half tri. Yu are rite also, about their being sure footed, iv'e known them tu kick a man, twise in a sekund, 10 feet oph.

"*Gertrude.*" — Yure inquiry stumps me, the darndest. The more i think on it, the more i kant tell. Az near az i kan rekolek now, i think i dont kno. Much mite be ced both ways, and neether wa be rite. Upon the whole i rather reckon i wud, or i wuddent, jist az i thought best, or otherwise.

"*Plutark.*" — Yu'are mistaken, the Shakers dont marry. If young Shakers fall in luv tha are sot tu weeding onions, and that kures them forthwithly. I kant tell yu now, how much it dus kost tu jine the Shakers but i beleave the expenze used tu be, inkluding having yure hair cut and larning how tu danse, about $65,00. I disreckoleckt what their religun iz, but if mi memry sarves me rite, it iz making almitey good brooms, and sellin devilish poor grape cuttings, for 75 cents a foot.

"*Sportsman.*"—Yure inquiry iz not edzackly in

mi line, but i haste tu repli, as follers, to wit: The rite length tu cut oph a dog's tale haz never yet bin fully diskovered, but iz undoubtedly somewhare bak ov hiz ears, provided yu git the dog's consent. N. B.— It aint absolutely necessara the dog's consent should be in riteing.

"*Kate.*"— I think Lord Biron waz the author ov the lines yu speke ov; 'twas either him or 'twas Captain Kid, one or tother. Biron waz dredful limber at riteing potri, so waz Kidd, but Biron waz the limberest.

V.

A TABLOWS IN 4 ACKS.

Ack Fust.— Enter a lap dorg, carrying a boarding skool miss in his arms, about 16 hands high — it makes the dorg puff — the dorg lays down the boarding skool miss, and orders mint juleks for 2, with the usual suckshun. The dorg begins tew loll, the boarding skool miss tells him "tew dri up," (in French,) and the dorg sez "he be darned if he will," (in Dorg.) [Grate sensashun among the awjence, with cries, "put him out!"] Finally a compromize iz affected, the boarding skool miss kisses the dorg, with tears in his eyes. Konlusion — Lap dorg diskovers a wicked flee at work on his tale — pursues him — round and round tha go — dorg a leettle ahead — sumbody hollers out, "mad dorg!" — boarding skool girl faints standing — the curtin drops.

Ack number 2.—Curtin highsts — sevral blind men in the distanse, looking thru a key whole — one ov them sez, "he don't see it!" A shanghi ruseter cums out, with epaulets on, and crows Yankee Doodle — musik bi the band. The shanghi lays an egg on the stage, about the size ov a wasps nest, and then limps oph, very much tired and redused. Curtin falls agin.

Ack number 3.—Curtin rizes sloly — big bolona sarsage on a tabel — bolona sarsage lifts up her hed, and begins tew bark — band plays "Old Dorg Tray." Cat cums in — cat's tail begins tew swell bad — bolona sarsage and cat haz a fite — tha fite 14 rounds — the stage iz covered with cats and dorgs. Konlusion — tha awl jine hands, and walk tew the foot lights — an old Bull Tarrier reads the President's call for "300 000 more" — band plays "Go in Lemons!" — a bell rings, and the curtin drops."

Ack number 4.—A scene on the Eri kanall — a terribel storm rages — the kanall acks bad — sevral line botes go down hed fust, with awl their boarders on board — kant make a lee shore — tha drag their ankers — sum ov the kaptins tri tew pra, but moste ov them hav the best luck at swareing — the water iz strewd with pots and kittles — sevral ov the cook maids swim ashore, with their cook stoves in their teeth — tha hav tew draw oph the kanal tew stop the storm. Konlusion — men are seen along on the banks ov the kanall spearing ded hosses and eels — band plays "a life on the oshun wave." Amid tremduous applauze the curtin falls, and the awjence disperce, single file.

Josh Billings' advice, and Answers to Correspondents.—*See pages* 19, 20

VI.

FEMALE EDDIKASHUN.

Thare iz so mutch ced about the importanze ov female eddikashun, now a daze, that a near-sighted person wud suppoze that wimmin, was running tu waist. The more that wimmin ar elevated, the more men ar histed up too, so tha sa, and them who maik this statement, ain't fur from out ov the wa. fur men hav bin clus after the wimmin, ever sinse humin beins waz perpetrated. Dear reader, dear, don't be maid a fool uv, by beleaving for the space ov a half-grown seckond, that Josh Billings, (more properly Joshua Billings, Esq.,) don't love, respeck, adore, and worship the sex, and ain't willing tu fite, even with the belly-ake onto him, two hundred pounds ov any kind ov man, in behalf ov enny vartuous, and worthy, or even good-looking woman.

I beleave in femail eddikashun, clear up tu the handle, provided the woman hankers for it, but if she don't hanker for it, i kant see why she shud be histed up into a posishun, where men has got to cease luving her, just in proposhun az tha are asked to wonder at her. Tha tell us that thare aint enny posishun that man kan fill, but what wimmin kan fill it tu ; but iz that enny reson why it iz best to prove it. I haven't enny doubt, that you could eddicate wimmin so muchly, that tha wouldn't kno enny more about getting dinner, than sum ministers ov the gospil kno about preaching, and while tha mite translate one ov Virgils ecklogs tu a spot, tha couldn't translate a baby out ov a kradle, without letting it cum apart.

I hold that natur haz its laws, and programmy, all the wa down, from the biling over ov a volkano tu the wiggle ov a lam's tale.— Suppose you shud take 100 yung injuns and eddikate them tu the highest pint, and then turn them luce ! 95 ov them wud throw a blanket ontu their shoulders, bid fairwell tu civilizashun, and dive intu the wildnerness; the uther 5 wud wander about among the pail faces, az far from hum az a Bufferlo wud be among a herd ov short tailed durhams. I believe in femail eddikashun, but i had ruther a woman cud beet me nussing a baby than tu feel that she cud beet me or enny other man in a stump speech or a lektur on veteranara praktiss.

If Billings understands human natur, and he thinks he duz, thare aint nothing that a true woman luvs more than the hole ov a man's harte; and, in order tu git this, she haz got tu kno less than he duz, or maik him think so. I thank the lord that thare aint menny wimmin in the wurld who want tu know evry thing. I kalkerlate that 9 out ov evry 10 ov the wimmin who luv their huzbands and glory in their children, will sa that tha had ruther be looked down upon in luving tenderniss than tu be looked up tu in silent aw.

If Josh Billings haz ced a wurd, in what he haz now rit, wich iz kalkulated tu damp the arder ov one single aspirin' woman, he iz reddy tu shed tears, but i hav alwus thort that the very highly eddikated wimmin work best in single harniss. In konklusion, i sa, elevate the wimmin, but if their heds and their hartes bekum antagonicks in the operashun, i shall continner tu think that luv, swapped for wizdom, iz a doutful gain to the wimmin and a pozatif loss to us poor mail-claid devils. Mi christian friends, ajew!

VIII.

DEPOZETIONS.

Josh Billings being duly sworn deposes as follows.

That, John Brown haz halted a fu days for refreshment.

That, moste men had ruther sa a smart thing than tew dew a good one.

That, baksliding iz a big thing, espeshila on ice.

That, a live traitor smells wuss than a ded one.

That, there iz 2 things in this life for which we are never fully prepared, and that iz twins.

That, yu kant judge a man bi hiz religgun

eny more than yu kan judge hiz shurt bi the size ov the collar and ristbands.

That, the devil iz alwus prepared tew see kompany.

That, it iz treating a man like a dog tew cut him opb short in hiz narrative.

That, "ignoranse iz bliss," ignoranse of sawing wood, for instanse.

That, menny will fale tew be saved simpla bekause tha haint got ennything tew saive.

That, the vartues ov woman are awl her own, but her frailities hav bin taught her.

That, dry *pastors* are the best for flocks; flocks ov sheep i mean.

That, men ov genius are like eagles, tha live on what tha kill, while men ov talents are like crows, tha live on what haz bin killed for them.

That, some peoples are fond ov bragging about their ansesstors, and their grate descent, when in fack, their *grate descent* iz jist what's the matter ov them.

That, a woman kant keep a sekret nor let ennybody else keep one.

That, "a little larning iz a dangerous thing; this iz az tru az it iz common.

That, sider brandee taken inwardly in large quantitys iz good — for a rat hole.

That, a grate menny folks have bin eddikated oph from their feet.

VIII.

WAR AND ARMY PHRAZES.

"A suckcessful Rade,"—cutting oph a turnpike within the enama's lines, and bringing in a blind mule, and 2 niggers tu board.

"Reserv'd Korps,"—this i take it means our ophisers; who die at the tavern stands, and are stuffed, and cent home tu berry.

"Bace of supplize,"— Unkle Samuel's pocket-Book.

"Pickitts,"—these are surplus chaps, who ar cent out tu borry turbacker, and to see if the kussed rebels hav got enny pass.

"An Armstise,"—giving the enema tu chances tu git licked instead ov one.

"Militara Stratergee,"—trying to reduse a swamp by ketching the bilyus fever out ov it.

"Lite Hoss Calvary,"—picked men who ride the hosses tu drink, when tha git thin.

"Rekrutin Ophisers,"—individuals who are cent into the rural destriks, on a furlong, to rekrute — themselfs.

"Armee Rashuns,"—back pay, and preserved beef!

"Quartring on the enemee," this phrase is defunkted, bekaze its contraree tu Hoyle.

"War Hoops,"—jist the things fur a hot da, the injuns used tu hav them.

"Corte Marshall,"—where tha tri the misdemeners out ov an ophiser, so that he'll du to promoat.

"Forage Partee,"—Them who goes out to kech a hastack, and gits lost in a forage ov treeze and haint been herd from sinse.

"On tu Richmond,"—that's tu sa if the kussed rebels will allow it.

"Parralel lines,"—are them kind of lines that never cum together.

"Militara necessita,"—ten ophisers and a gallon ov whiski to every three privates.

"Onluce the dogs ov war;"—but muzzle the darn kritters; if you don't, somebody will get hurt.

"War of Exterminashun,"—this fraze belongs holey tu the Kommissara Department.

"Advance Gard,"—this is a gard tha hav tu hav in our army tu keep our fellers from pichin in tu the enema frontwards.

"Rere Gard,"—this is a gard that hav tu keep our fellers, when tha are surrounded from pitching intu the enema backwards.

"Awl quiet on the Potermuck,"—this shows what perfect subjekshun our fellers are under.

IX.

PASHUNCE OV JOB.

Evryboddy iz in the habit ov bragging on Job, and Job did hav konsiderable bile pashunce, that's a fac, but did he ever keep a distrik skule for 8 dollars a month, and borde 'round? Did he ever reap lodged oats down hill in a hot da, and hav all hiz gallus buttons bust oph at once? Did he ever hav the jumpin teethake, and be made tu tend baby while hiz wife was over tu Perkinses tu a teasquall? Did he ever git up in the morning awful dri and turf it 3 miles befoar brekfast tu git a drink, and find that the man kep a tempranse hous? Did he ever undertaik tu milk a kicking hefer with a bushy tail, in fli time, out in the lot? Did he ever sot down onto a litter ov kittens in the old rockin cheer, with hiz summer pantyloons on without saing "damnashun!" If he cud du all theze things, and praze the Lord at the same time, all i hav got tu sa, iz, *Bully for Job!*

X.

FRIENDLY LETTER.

Friend Elias:—You ask me menny questions about the draft that bothers me. It iz curis how it duz act, but it waz jist so in scripter times, " 2 wimmin waz at a mill a grinding (corn i reckon), one waz took, and t'other want took." There aint enny dout but the draft iz for 3 years, or thereabouts, but i think a person would hav a rite to sell out hiz chanse at enny time during the 3 years, or thereabouts, for a premium, provided he could show tu the government that he waz conscientzly oppozed tu hard tak and bilyus fever.

Again : Aleyens aint liable for the draft, espeshila if tha cum from the city ov Ireland, and hav bin in the habit, for the laste 5 years, ov voting the democratic ticket.

Againly : Widder-wimmin, and their only son iz exempt, provided the widder's husband haz alreddy sarved 2 years in the war, and iz willing tu go agin; i beleave the supreme corto haz desided this thing forever.

Onse more: If a drafted man shud run awa with hiz draft, he proberly wouldn't ever be allowed to stand a draft agin, this looks severe at fust site, but the more yu look at it, the more yu can see the wisdom into it.

Onse morely: Xempts are thoze who hav bin drafted into the stait prizzen, for triing tu git an honest living bi supporting 2 wives at onst; also, all them people who are crazee, and unsound on the goose; also, all nusepaper korrespondents and fools in general.

Onse morely again: No substidude will be acksepted, who iz less than 3, or more than 10 feet high, he must know how to chaw terbacker and drink whiskee, and must'nt be afeered ov the itch nor the rebels. Moral Karakter aint required, the government furnishes that, and rashuns.

Conclusively: No person kan be drafted but twice in 2 different plases without hiz consent, but awl men haz a rite tu be drafted at least onst; i don't think even a rit ov habus corpus could deprive a man ov this laste, blessed privlege.

XI.

AFFURISMS.

Truth iz the onla thing I kno ov that kant be improved upon.

If yu want tew git a sure krop, and a big yield for the seed, sow wilde oats.

An insult tew one man iz an insult tew aul men.

Cunning is curiosity satisfied, and curiosity satisfied iz wisdom.

Wize men don't expeck tu do away with the visisitudes ov life, they onla expeck tew blunt the edge ov them.

Yu kan gorge avaris, but ambishun knows no gorge but the grave.

A sarkastic wit iz a kind ov human pole-cat.

If thare is enny thing on this arth that angels kant imitate 'tis a vartuous yung man trampling temtashun under hiz feet.

I had rather be a reseiver ov stolen goods than the keeper ov men's sekrets.

Fame iz jist about az mutch use tew a ded man as 5.20's wud be, interest payable in goold.

Sum people hav the power ov saing a good deal in a fu words, while others hav the power ov saing a little in a good menny wurds.

Slander iz played on a tin horn, while truth steals forth like the dieing song ov a lute.

Yu kan judge ov sum men's karakters onla bi what they eat and drink.

"Truth iz stranger than ficshun" — that iz tew sum folks.

I hav found a grate menny things in this wurld that waz *free* — free az a well tew git into, but like a rat trap, not edzackly free tu git out ov.

"Meet me bi moonlite alone," iz awl well enuff under sum circumstances; but moonlite me for meat alone, iz not so well ennuff, under enny circumstances.

I don't kno ov but one thing on arth that kan improve a good wife, and that iz buty.

After you hav made up yure mind jist what you are going to du, then iz a good time tew dew it.

We often hear ov men, who hav cum within an inch ov dieing, and i haint enny dout thare iz sum, that evry boddy wuld lik tew hear had cum within an inch ov bein born.

"The lapse ov ages," iz a pleasant thing tew dwell upon, but after awl, verry mutch depends upon the ages ov the laps.

It iz not differkult tew find augers that wont bore, but yu seldom cum across a bore that wont auger.

"Faith that iz founded on an arnest and truthful convickshun, iz butiful tu behold; but faith that iz founded simpla on courage, aint enny thing more than good grit.

XII.

JOSH BILLINGS ON CATS.

I hav studdyed cats clussly for years, and hav found them adikted tew a wild state. Tha haint got affekshun, nor vartues ov enny kind, tha will skratch their best friends, and wont ketch mice unless tha are hungry. It haz bin sed that tha are good tu make up into sassages; but this iz a grate mistake, i hav bin told bi a sassage maker that tha dont kompare with dogs. Thare is one thing sartin, tha are verry anxious tew liv, yu ma turn one inside out, and hang him up bi the tale, and az soon az yu are out ov sight, he will manage tew turn back summerset and cum around awl rite in a fu days. It iz verry hard wurk tew looze a cat. If one gits carried oph in a bag bi mistake a grate ways into the kuntry, tha wont sta lost onla a short time, but soon appear tew make the family happy with their presence. Old maids are very

Josh Billings on Cats.—*See page* 40.

fond ov cats, for the reason i suppose that cats never marry if tha hav ever so good a chanse. Thare iz one thing about cats i dont like, if yu step on their tales by acksident tha git mad rite oph, and make a grate fuss about it. Thare iz anuther thing about them which makes them a good investment for poor folks. A pair ov cats will yield each year, without any outlay, something like eight hundred per cat. It iz a verry singular fack that cats dont like a millpond, i never knu one tew git drowned bi acksident. Tha luv cream, but it seems tew be agin their religgun tew tutch soap. Cats and dogs have never bin able tew agree on the main question, tha both seem tew want the affirmatiff side to onst. I think if i could hav mi way thare wouldn't be enny more cats born unless tha could sho a certifikate ov good moral karakter. Thare is one more thing about cats which seems tew me tew be awl affektashun, and that iz making sich a devlish noise under a fellers window nights, and then kall it musik. If i waz tew hav mi choise between a cat and a striped snake, i would take the snake bekause I could git rid ov the snake bi letting him go. Thare aint no sartin wa tew kill a cat, if yu git one wurked up into sassage, and yu think yu are awl right, jist az likely az not tha will cum to and take off a whole lot of good sassage with them.—Theze are mi views about cats, rather hastily hove together, and if i haint said enuff agin them it iz onla bekause i lack the informashun.

XIII.

REMARKS.

Impudense iz the affek ov tew *little* knollege, and modesta, iz az often the affek ov tew *mutch*.

We dont question a persons rite tew be a fule, but if he klaims wisdom, we kompare it with our own.

Not one man in a thousand iz known while living, yet awl expeck tew be well remembered, when tha are ded.

Men are very often ashamed tu tell the truth, bekause tha dont kno how.

Moste ov the advise we reseave from others, iz not so mutch an evidense ov their affeckshun for us, az it iz an evidense ov their affeckshun for themselves.

Aul ov us komplain ov the shortness ov life, yet we all waste more time than we uze.

Aboutaz good a wa az enny tew be happee, iz tew pity thoze who are below us, and forgit that there iz enny boddy above us

Wit iz a pleasant surprize ov Truth.

No man haz a rite tu be proud till he bekums entirely vartuous. and then he wont feel like being proud.

The power ov oratory lays more in the manner, than in the matter; yu kant reduse it tew riting, enny more than yu kan pla a streak ov lightning on a hand organ.

Sum folks when tha fite, will throw the fust brik bat tha kan git hold ov, jist so sum folks will du when tha argy.

Epitaff — here lies John Ferguson, Esq., died wurth half a million — less the kingdom ov heaven.

Avaris eats up all the good things in a man, and then feeds on his vices.

XIV.

JOSH BILLINGS ADDRESSES THE "FEMAIL BILLINGSVILLE SOWING SOSIETY."

FELLER SISTERS :—When I caste mi eye on a sirkle of luvely wimmin bizzy with their needles, mi harte seems tew stretch clean akross mi buzzum. And when i reflek for a minnit, that tha are tew work for nothing, and find themselfs, and that a yung heathin stans reddy yelping around the corner, for the very shirt tha are wurking on, it duz seem tu me, that i cud shout hozzanner for 3 weeks on a strech. Feller Sisters, yu kan kount on Josh Billings az a frend; he luves charitee, az a pup hankers for nu milk; his verry natur looks out onto the horizen ov the poor folks, jist as the lite ov a tin lantern shines akross a bog meddow. And he sees the little bare bak yung ones shivering for a krust ov bread, and hungry for a shirt; then he looks at the Sisters, a talking and sowing, and sowing and talking, and he kounts a hole parcil ov little shirts on the tabil, and then he thinks ov the widders cruise, and the bred hove onto the waters, menshioned in the good Book, and he feels jist az tho he wud like tew own awl the femail sowing sosieties in the wurld hisself, and put hiz hole fortin in the little reddy made cottin shirt bizziness. Oh Charitee! Oh Chartee! When Josh Billings communes with you, he feals az tho he had jist been tried out, and sot awa tew cool. Feller Sisters don't be skeered, let the ritch and the hawty stik up their nozes, and let the eddicated larf. Josh wud like no better fun than jiss to bet his 9 dollars, that enny Sister, in full communion with this ere sowing sosiety, who puts in full time, and cuts the cotting tew advantage, wil git her final reward. Tew konklude, Feller Sisters, pitch in; remember Mr. Lots wife, she that was salted for looken bak. Cum together arly, and oftin, buy yure cottin by the pease; be keerful how yu deal out youre shirts, for thare iz evry now and then a bogus heathin. Stan bi yure konstitushion, and bi laws, dew awl this, and the " Femail Billingsville Sowing Sosiety " will go down tew futer prosterita, like a wide-awake torchlite possession. I bid yu tenderla ajew.

XV.

NOSHUNS.

Yankee Noshuns.

In gazeing at the different kind ov noshuns that prevale jist now, we are struck with the vitality, and permiskuousness, ov the Yankee noshuns. These are a kind ov noshuns that reside in Nu England, but travel awl over the world. They are for the present known az the lead gimblet, the basswood sperm-kandle, and the sole leather juise harp noshun, relieved at times, by the hickory lossenge, the charkole led pensil, and the lard bears ile noshun, and okasionally interlined, tew keep up the appetite, with paper razor straps, plaster-paris sheep shears, and the sour milk opedeldock noshun, which iz warranted tew kure the attack ov a 50 cent shinplaster, in 4 seckunds; to which has lately bin added, pewter jak knives, with pork rhine handles, and itch intement, made out ov strong butter, and lamblak. Yankee noshuns are the affek ov tew mutch genius.

Hoss Noshuns.

It iz really curis how folks differ in their noshuns about hosses, sum wants a bob-tailed hoss, and sum dont, sum wants a bay, and sum wants a yaller, and sum wants any culler so bad that they hav tew be sent tew state prizon, tew be healed ov their pashion for the nobel animal, the hoss. I knu ov one old feller who waz very noshunal, he wouldn't hav a hoss only jist so high, he never stabled him, and let him git hiz own fodder, he kept him for 47 years, and the hoss outlived him, the last time I saw the hoss he waz alive, but poor az wood; the old feller called the hoss "saw-buck," and sed he waz sired bi carpenter, out ov a white ash skantling. Hoss noshuns are well enuff, but they never ought tew be allowed tew interfere with a man's final salvashun.

Rum Noshuns.

Perhaps thare iz no subjek that moste men agree on so well bi the gallon, but when it comes down tew a drink, that they are so full ov noshuns about, az their rum. I hav seen lots ov old-fashioned people, who never thought ov drinking tanzy, unless they

Josh Billings on trotting horses.—*See page* 63.

put rum into it, and wouldn't no more drink a gin-coktale without nutmeg on the top ov it, than they would skim milk. Then agin their iz sum who must hav Jamaka, or the bronkeetis, one, or tuther; and sum who must hav the belly-ake 3 or 4 times a day, or they kant relish brandee and sugar. But thare waz one beardless boy, over whose hed skase 14 summers had melted, who beats them awl, he aktually hove a fust class mint julek away, and called for anuther, jist bekause it wouldn't suk fast enuff, through the straw; I call this letting a man's good sense git the better ov his judgment. Rum noshuns are like gitting struk with litening, the theory iz well enuff, but the praktis is a bad one tew git into.

Religious Creed Noshuns.

The idee that thare iz onla one way tew git tew Heaven iz awl rong, but the idee that there iz but one Heaven tew git tew, iz awl right. Az a gineral thing nations go tew war for the most ornary things, so men will fite the wust kind, for a religious noshun, that they hain't got the fust smell of. I dont care, for mi part, whether a man iz a piscopaleyen, or a soft shell baptiss, nor I don't think the Lord duz nuther. Religious creed noshuns for man, are like the scent the foxes leave for the hounds, the less thare iz ov it, the more kerful the dorg hunts, and the less likely he iz tew take enny uther trak.

XVI.

SAYINS.

If yu hav got a real good wife, kepe perfectly still, and thank God evry twenty minnitts for it.

A man with one idee alwus put me in mind ov an old goose a tryin to hatch out a paving stun.

"Honesta is the best polisy," but dont take mi wurd for it, tri it.

Menny a book has bin writ, which proved tu be an obituara notis ov the author.

Tha tells us "that munny is the rute ov all evil;" and then tell us "tu rute hog or di."

A man running for offiss puts me in minde ov a dog that's lost — he smells ov everybody he meets, and wags hisself all over.

Look out, galls! the Jack of hartes is alwus a nave.

Gravity is very often mistakin for wisdum, but thare is as much differ as thare is between a gide board and the man who maid it.

Evra man has a goose that lays golden eggs, if he only nu it.

XVII.

ANSWERS TO CONTRIBUTORS.

"*Lines tu a sleeping infant*, bi Alice," receaved. Tha are tender, dredful tender, almost tu tender, tu keep thru this hot spel; yu hav talons ov the highest order, but yu must kross yure t's, or yu kant suckeed in portri; good bi Alice!

"*Reverie ov a Bachelor,*" Anonimous.—Received, and kontents noted. Thare iz only one trubble with this produckshun, which time will correkt, and that iz, "it wont du at all for our collums," respekfully declined, (on the part ov the edditurs, by J. B.) on account ov its length and thickness.

"*The Sea, the roarin Sea.*"—A sublime standzas, wurth at least 7 dollars, intended, undoubtedly, for *The Atlantic Monthly,* and cent tu us bi mistake, we wud like tu accept it, but dassent, fur fere folks mite sa we stole it.

"*Will yu Kiss me Dearest*," Bi Mary Ann.—Acksepted. We take all them kind ov chanses. The potri ain't fust rate, but we expect the kissin kan't be beat, till then, fair Maid ajew!

"*A gealogikal synopsorum ov the heavenly spears*," Bi Paul Vernon — Will appere in our nex issu. This writer haz attaked a subjeck ov grate differkilty, with the biggest kind ov energee, and haz suckceeded; his thesis is admirable, hiz argyment iz clus, and his stile is camphene. We sa "Mount Vernon! on eagil wings, beyond the klouds, and paint yure name rite over the top ov the door that leads tu glory, Mount Vernon, mi boy!" We predick grate poplarity for this writer, if he aint kut oph by a frost.

"*A Prairie on fire*," Bi Diogoneze.—Rejeckted to onst. Tu hot for the sezon — cool artikles take the best now. It made me swet tu rede the manuskrip. "Dont despair Diogoneze," if yu find literature aint yure stile, tri sawing wood; iv'e known hundreds ov men make a dust sawing wood, who want worth a cuss tu write for the nusepapirs.

"*Wait a little longer*," Bi Eugene.—This potri wants greasing. Thare aint nothin so eaza tu rite az potri, if yu know how. Our advise tu this author iz tu take pills, and if tha dont release him ov his potri, he kan konklude he haz got the potri dizeaze the natral wa, and iz liable tu brake out at sumtime.

In konklusion, Fustly, we would sa tu moste writers, " write often, and publish seldom." Secondly, tu sum writers, " write seldom and publish seldemmer."

XVIII.

THE DEVIL'S PUTTY AND VARNISH.

When a man cums tew the konklusion that he would like tew kill sumboddy at thirty paces, he imagines that he haz bin wronged, and sends hiz best friend a challenge tew fite a dewell; tha meet, and an elegant murder iz committed; the cracks, in this transaktion are puttyed up, and then varnished over, bi being kalled, "*an affair ov honnor.*" When a man robs a saving bank, or goes tew urope on the last steamer, with the stolen reseipts ov a sanitary kommittee in his pocket, a kommittee ov investigashun are got together tew examine the stait ov affairs, and unanimously report "*a diskrepansy in hiz akounts.*" 2 yung men hire a hoss and buggy at a livri stable, and go into the kuntry on Sunda. Tha stop at the fust tavern tha meet, and invest in sum ardent speerits. They stop agin pretty soon, and histe in sum more ardent speerits. The more tha histe in, the more tha drive, till bi and bi a devilish bridge tips them over into a devilish gutter that sumboddy haz left bi the side ov the road, and tha are awl killed, including the hoss and buggy. This is kalled a "*Fatal acksident.*" A man and hiz wife are living in the middle ov joy and consolashun, tha are surrounded on awl sides bi a yung and interesting familee, their bread iz cut thin, and buttered on both sides and the edges, but the destroyer enters the family, the wife wants a nu silk gown, the man sez he "be d—d if she duz," and she "be d—d if she dont." One word brings on another, till tha fite, both ov them lose awl the hair in their heds, and 2 full setts ov false teeth, the thing ends in a divorse, the man runs awa tew Australia bi the overland route, the woman marry's a cirkus rider at 40 Dollars a month, the children are adopted bi sum sunda school, and are brought up on homopathy. This furnishes a collum and a half in the nusepaper, under the hed ov "*Disturbanse ov the marrid relation.*" A youth ov 21 summer begins life with 36 thousand dollars. Sevral fast hosses belong tew him, there iz sevral fast wimmin that he belongs tew, awl the tavern keepers are hiz patrons, faro banks are bilt for hiz amuzement, consolidated lotterys are chartered on purpiss tew make him happee; nothing iz left undun tew make him feel good. He wakes up about the 25th ov next May, without a dollar in hiz pocket, and a host ov warm friends on hiz hands, without enny visible means ov supporting them. He takes an akount ov stock, he buys a pint ov rum and 4 yards ov bed kord, the one makes him limber, while the other makes him stiff. The putty and varnish in this kase iz, "*Driven tew desperashun on akount of finanshui preshure.*" A rale rode trane stands snorting in front ov the depoe, the last bel iz ringing, the kars are full ov souls that belong tew different individuals, the konducktor iz full ov Bourbon, that belongs tew the devil, the engineer labors under an attack ov Jamaka for the broketis, the switchmen likes a leetle good old rye, the kars diskount 45 miles a hour, 2 trains tri tew pass each other on the same track; it kant be did suckcessfully; the mangled and ded are kounted bi skores, a searching investigashun takes plase, the community iz satizfied, bekause it waz, "*an unavoidable katastrophe.*" The Devil furnishes putty and varnish, free ov expense, tew hide the frauds and guilt ov men. Aul ov which iz respekfully committed Bi

JOSH BILLINGS.

XIX.

MANIFEST DESTINY.

Manifest destiny iz the science ov going tew the devil, or enny other place before yu git thare. I may be rong in this centiment, but that iz the way it strikes me, and i am so put together that when enny thing strikes me i immejiately strike back. Manifest destiny mite perhaps be blocked out agin az the condishun that man and things find themselfs in with a ring in their nozes and sumboddy hold ov the ring. I may be rong agin, but if i am, awl i hav got tew sa iz, i don't kno it, and what a man don't kno ain't no damage tew enny boddy else. The tru way that manifess destiny had better be sot down iz, the exact distance that a frog kan jump down hill with a striped snake after him; i dont kno but i may be wrong onst more, but if the frog don't git ketched the destiny iz jist what he iz a looking for.

When a man falls into the bottom ov a well and makes up hiz minde tew stay thare, that ain't manifess destiny enny more than having yure hair cut short iz; but if he almoste gits out and then falls down in agin 16 foot deeper and brakes off his neck twice in the same plase and dies and iz buried thare at low water, that iz manifess destiny on the square. Standing behind a bull in fly time and gitting kicked twice at one time, must feel a good deal like manifess destiny. Being about 10 seckunds tew late tew git an express train, and then chasing the train with yure wife, and an umbreller in yure hands, in a hot day, and not getting az near tew the train az you waz when yu started, looks a leetle like manifess destiny on a rale rode trak. Going into a tempranse house and calling for a little old Bourbon on ice, and being told in a mild way that "the Bourbon iz jist out, but they hav got sum gin that cost 72 cents a gallon in Paris," sounds tew me like the manifess destiny ovmoste tempranse houses.

Mi dear reader, don't beleave in manifess destiny untill yu see it. Thare iz such a thing az manifess destiny, but when it occurs it iz like the number ov rings on the rakoon's tale, ov no grate consequense onla for ornament. Man wan't made for a machine, if he waz, it waz a locomotiff machine, and manifess destiny must git oph from the trak when the bell rings, or git knocked higher than the price ov gold. Manifess destiny iz a disseaze, but it iz eazy tew heal; i hav seen it in its wust stages cured bi sawing a cord ov dri hickory wood. I thought i had it onse, it broke out in the shape ov poetry; i sent a speciment ov the disseaze tew a magazine, the magazine man wrote me nex day as follers,

"*Dear Sur:* Yu may be a dam phule, but yu are no poeck. Yures, in haste."

XX.

ANSWERS TO CONTRIBUTORS.

Perkins — I hav red yure peace, on "Wimmins Rites," thru, and thru, and must say that i luv it. In mi opinyun, wimmin haz a rite to tu dew enny thing well, but saw wood; sawin wood, ain't their stile; speshially if the sawbuk iz a high one, it must mortify them the wust wa.

Harrold.— Yure genus iz not fully born yet, when it gits awl born, i think yu will be a poeck. Yu hav got imaginashun enuff tew keep a livery stable. Yure landguage iz a leetle too florid; did you ever travel in Florida? Tri agin — I notis one ov yure lines, haz 10 feet into it, and the nex one, haz only got 9 feet, six inches. Sum poiks air born, and sum are manafaktured; the manafaktured ones, are the moste stiddyest, tha aint so ap tew hanker after mint juleps. Yu ought to go up garrett when yu praktis, moste awl good poeckry haz bin rit up garrett.

Hard Road.—Yure essa has sum good hits intu it, but iz not jis the thing for a religus nuzepaper, like ours; send it tu " Wilkes Spirit," a paper that knows how tu talk hoss. I will merely suggess, that pedigree iz not important for a fast trotting hoss; if he kan trot fast, never minde the pedigree. Thare iz a grate menny fast men, even, who haint got no pedigree. Thare aint mutch art in driving a trotting hoss, jist hold them bak hard, and holler them ahead hard, thats awl. A hoss will trot the fastest down hill, espeshila, if the briching brakes. Kuller is no kriterion. I hav seen awful mean hosses, ov awl kullers, excep green, i never cee a mean one ov this kuller. Hosses liv tew an honarabil old age, and i hav often seen them, that apeared fully prepared for deth. Heathins are alwus kind tew hosses; it iz only among christian people, that a hoss haz tew trot 3 mile heats, in a hot da, for $25,000 in kounterfit munny.

XXI.

ON DOGS.

> When fickle frends and fickler fortin fales,
> Dogs, unfickle still, for you will wag their tales.

Dogs are various in kind, and thanks tew an all-wise Providence, tha are various in number. Tha are the onla animil ov the brute perswashun, who hav voluntary left a wilde stait ov natur, and cum in under the flag ov man. Tha are not vagabones bi choise, and luv tew belong tu sumbody. This fac endears them tew us, and i hav alwas rated the dog az about the seventh cusin tew the humain specious. Tha kant talk, but tha kan lick yure hand, this shows that their hearts iz in the plase where uther folks' tungs iz. Dogs in the lump are useful, but tha are not alwas proffittable in the lump. The Nufoundlin dog is useful tew saive chldiren from drowning, but yu hav got tew hav a pond or water, and children running around kareless, or else the dog aint profitable. Thare aint nothing maid boarding a Nufoundlin dog. Rat Tarries air useful tew kech rats, but the rats aint proffittable after yu hav keched them. The Shepard dog is useful tew drive sheep, but if yu hav got tew go and buy a flock ov sheep, and pay more than tha are wurth, jist to keep the dog bizzy, the dog aint proffittable, not mutch. Lap dogs are very useful, but if yu dont hold them in yure lap awl the time, tha aint proffittable at all. Bull dogs are extremely useful, but yu hav got tew keep a bull too, or else yu kant make ennnything on the dog. The Coach dog iz one ov the moste usefullest ov dogs i kno ov, but yu hav got to hav a coach, (and that aint alwus pleasant) or yu kant realize from the dog. Thus we cee, that while dogs are ginerally useful, thare are times, when tha aint ginerally proffittable. I dont really luv a Yaller dog, nor a mad dog, but with these two unfortunate excepshuns, it is dredful hard work for me to sa a hard word agin a dog; the wag ov their tails is what takes me. Enny man who will abuze a dog, neadn't ask me to luv him, or pra for him. Enny man who will abuze a dog will abuse a woman, and enny man who will abuse a woman is thirty-five or forty miles miles meaner than — a pale paller dog. These are my centiments, and i shant change them, until i receive notice that the camel has smoothed down the hump on his back, and the sarpent ceases tew wiggle when he wanders.

XXII.

SAYINGS OF JOSH BILLINGS.

I think the fools do more hurt in this world than the raskals.

The prinsipal differense between a luxury and a necesaary iz, the prise.

Awl men hav cunning, and sum men hav wisdum.

If I aint mistaken, the best wa tew git religion, iz tew git honesta, and truth, and a sprinklin ov morality fust, and see how they agree with us.

What a man spends in this life, he saves : what he dont git want ment for him, and what he saves, he loozes.

Fame iz like a crop ov kanada thissells, very eazy tew sow, but hard tew reap.

"Familiarity breeds contempt." this iz so — jist as soon az we git familiarized with castor ile, for instance we contempt it.

Life is short, but it iz long enuff to ruin enny man who wants tew be ruined.

When the soul iz in grief, it iz taking root, and when it iz in smiles, it iz taking wing.

The grate art in writing well, iz tew kno when tew stop.

Every time yu forgive a man yu weaken him, and strengthen yurself.

Mi private opinion iz. that i should prefer boned fish tew boned turkey.

"Giv the devil his due," but be very kerful that thare aint mutch due him.

It haz bin obsarved, "that corporashuns haint got enny souls." Thare iz excepshuns tew this rule, for i kno ov several that hav got the meanest kind ov souls.

After a man has rode fast onse, he never wants tew go slow agin.

"Sparks fly upward." Old maids will pleaze make a note ov this.

"What will it proffit a man, if he gain the whole wurld, and loze his own soul? i answer, nothing: but thare are cases, whare thare wouldn't be enny loss tew speek ov.

"Think twice before yu speak onse," but don't think, "d—n it."

Thare iz onla one thing that i blame Adam for, and that iz, when he had the onla woman on arth, he didn't git her warranted.

XXIII.

FASHION.

Fashion is a compound mixtur ov much taist, and sum vanitee. The taist that is into it, saives it from ridikule. Fashun iz just az necessara tu govern men and wimmin with, az sivil law; in fack menny folks wud ruther brake a statu than tu ware a cut tale tu short, or a bunnet tu obtuze.

Exsentrisity iz one thing, and fashun iz anuther thing. We haint got no more rite tu laff at fashun, than we hav tu laff at vittels. What a man, or woman eats, if it iz well cooked, iz all rite, and what tha ware, if it iz well cooked, is ditto. — After fashuns hav had their da, then iz the time tu despize them; just so it iz with vittels; cold vittels for instanze.

Nobody iz tu blame for old fashuns. If our grate grand mother shud meet our present mother, both ov them dressed in the fashun ov their respektif daze, tha wud go tu kalling each other old Fools, and we should stan by, and offer tu bet on it. If evry boddy had a fashun ov their own, it wud make az mutch trubble az a shinplaster kurrensy. Them that sett the fashun, aught tu be vartuous and big minded, bekauze the morals ov a people are just about az mutch inflooensed by fashun az tha are by religun. In them daze, when tha had no partiklar fashun, tha didn't hav partiklar enny thing else. It iz more evidense ov vanitee to rejek fashun, than it iz tu adopt it.

Evra boddy, more or lessly, hankers after fashun. Fashun makes the poor ambishus, and it makes the rich affabil; it makes the the vartuous cheerful, and it makes the humbly kind ov handsum, and thare iz no reson why it shud make the modest bold, enny more than elegense shud make the butiful wicked. Thare has alwus bin wolfs in sheeps clothing, and fashun will okasionally be used for the same purpis, but that aint enny reson why mutton aint good, nor why fashun shud be hipokrasy. Bekauze sum peopil are slaves tu fashun only proves its power, and yu will find that thoze who are its slaves are ginerally free from moste ov the big sins that humin natur iz subjec tu. The big minded, and the noble, adopt fashun jist az tha du enny uther proper kustom, simpla bekause it iz the fashun.

It is tru that sum ov the fashuns are absurd, and it is tru that sum ov the vartues are absurd also. If a fashun kant be maid tu square itself tu the rules ov either good cense or good taist, it aint fashun, it is consait. A grate menny folks ced that whoops was a failure, but tha held their own, and grew nisely; tha are realy evra thing in a hot da. I shud like tu set in one all thru Juli and August; a feller wud be as cool as a dog's nose in a wire muzzel.

The essa is thru.

The occasional effect of Santa Cruz Rum on a gentleman of genial spirits.—*See page* 80.

XXIV.

REMARKS

Marrying a woman for her munny is vera mutch like setting a rat-trap, and baiting it with yure own finger.

"Between tew evils chuze the least." Brandee and gin, for instance, which will yu hav?

Perhaps sum philosophick mind kan tell me why the Jews never eat whats on the left side ov a baked goose.

If men had a good deal more faith than tha had kommon sense, moste ov them wud expek tu liv, as Eliger ov old did.

When a man's harte gits up into his hed, his charitces will smell tu mutch ov wisdom; and when his hed gits down into his harte, his wisdom smells tu much ov charitee.

I wud as soon take a ten dollar kounterfit bill on the Kodfish Bank ov Nufoundland, as tu marry a woman with false hare, false teeth or a false buzzum.

Men don't repli tu real sarkasm.

Ginowine proverbs ar like good kambrick needles — short, sharp, and shiny.

The fust man who was born inter the wurld, killed the sekund one, and i aint sure but it wud hav bin a good plan if the men had tuk their turns at killing ever sinse.

Art improves a diamond, but kant make one.

"Gra hares are honarabil," but I kno ov a grate menny gra *heds* that the devil will keep under a glas kase, tu sho the curous in theze matters.

XXV.

PROVERBIAL PIG.

Az the white rose wakens intu buty, so dus the white Pig cum tu gladden us. His ears are like the lilac leaf, played upon bi the young zephurs at eventide, his silkaness is the woof ov buty, and his figger is the outline ov lovlaness. His food is white nectar, drawn from the full fountain ov affecshun. He waxes fatter, and more slik, evra da, and hangs from the buzzum ov his muther like an image ov alabastur. He laffeth at forms, and curleth his tale still clusser, as his feast goeth on, then he riseth with gladness, and wandereth with his kindred, beside the still waters. His brothers and sisters are az like him as flakes ov snow, and all the day long, amung the red klover, and beneath the white thorn, he maketh his joy, and leadeth a life arkadian. His words are low musik, and his language the untutored freshness ov natur. His pastime is the history ov innersence, and his lessure is elaganse. He walketh whare grase leadeth, and gambles tew the dallianse ov dewy fragranse. He gathereth straws in his mouth, and hasteneth awa on errants ov gladness. He listeneth tu the reproof of biz parent; his ackshuns are the laws ov perliteness, and his logick is the power ov instinkt. His datime is pease and his evening is gentle forgitfullness. As he taketh on years, he loveth kool plases, and delveth in liquids, and stirreth the arth tew a fatness, and painteth hisself in dark cullers, a reffuge from flize, and the torments ov life. He forgetteth his parent, and bekumeth his own master, and larneth the mistery ov food, and groweth hugely. Men gaze at his porkyness, and kount his vallu bi pounds, and la in wate for him, and sacrifise him, and give his flesh salt for its safety. This is Pig life.

XXVI.

PROVERBS.

Preeching the gospel for nothin, is easy enuff, but preeching it fur 5 thousand a yere, and hav it sute, is anuther thing entirely.

A ded traitor makes a sweete korps.

Matches, ma be *made* in heavin, but tha ar ginerally *sold* down here.

Yu ma make a whissel out ov a pig's tale, but if you du, you'll find you've spilte a verry worthy tale, and got a devilish poor whissel.

I consait thare is this difference between bashfullness, and modesta, the one soon wares oph, the other never dus.

A vartuous, and ekonomikal, and knooing, and butiful woman is — *is*, all that kan be sed on the subjec.

Fitckshun is a kind ov haf wa hous, betwen the temples ov Truth and Fallshood, whare the good and the bad meet tu lie a little.

Praing, and Charitee, ought tu be dun on the sli.

The moste intensely butiful scene i ever perused, was a clene, fat, haf dressed baby, on the floor, kicking up its little heels, and pounding a lookin glass, and a gold watch together.

Munny is like promises, easier maid than kept.

The fules in this wurld make about as much trubble as the wicked du.

Misfortin and twins hardly ever cum singly.

XXVII.

ANSWERS TO CORRESPONDENTS.

Bolivar.— Yu are rite about it, courtin a yung widder iz no boys play. Yu hav got to stick and hang. Feed them well, and take them tu the circus, and go out into the avenu with a kupple ov blood ba lightning calculators, that's the wa! Dont waste enny time waiting for a full moon nuther. Widders luv oysters and gass lite the best. Dont flatter them much, but pitch in, and rush matters. Menny a widder has bin lost, bi fuleing around, gitting reddy tu court. Maids luv centiment, but widders luv muscle.

Fanny.— Pork and beans are good, that's a fack, but yu must go down suller and eat them, don't let ennybody cee yu du it. Sassage grease iz ap tu rise on the stummuk, and if yu eat raw onions, and dont swaller them hull, tha are ap tu make yure breth defensive, so tha sa. If yu want tew katch yure bo, run rite tuther wa, and skream a small-sized skream, and dont look bak till yu katch him. If yure bo wants tew marry yu, and yu ar enny whar near reddy, it iz a good genral rule tew let him du it.

David.—The best kind ov a dog tew hav for awl purposes iz a wooden one. Tha dont kost much, and aint liable tew git out ov repair. They are easy kep, and yu alwus kno whare tu find them. Tha aint kross tu children when yu step on their tales. Bi awl means git a small one. I never knu one ov this breed tu foller ennybody oph.

Citizen.—I think yu hav cum tu just konklusion from the premisis. Yu sa, " enny man who will chaw plug terbakker, will drink santa kruize rum; enny man who will drink santa kruize rum, will go tew the devil; and enny man who will go tu the devil, is mean enuff tu du enny thing." Bi thunder, i think yure more than $\frac{3}{4}$ rite, I will think the thing over clus, and if i find you are rite, i'll telegraff tew yu.

Richard,—Thare aint no sich thing az a munny aristokrat in this free Amerikan land ov freedum. If a man knows more than anuther man, he has got a rite tew throw his hed bak and brag onto it a little. But if a man haint got onla munny, he haint got no more rite tu brag onto it then he wud hav tu brag onto a big pile ov manure that wanted spreading.

Gipsey.—I kant giv yu enny partikler rule for riteing for the nuzepapers. Korrekt spelling iz the verry bowels ov suckcess. This art is onkomon hard tew obtain; but few ever reach it, and liv. If yu want yure name tew go down tu posterita untarnished, dont rite for the nusepapers, but go and hav yure name painted in red letters onto a board, and la it awa up garrett.

4*

XXVIII.

PROVERBS OF THE BILLINGS FAMILY.

Humin natur is the same all over the world, cept in Nu England, and thar its akordin tu sarcumstances.

A kodfish aristokrat alwus puts me in mind ov a drunken man a tryin tu walk a krack.

Rum is good in its plase, and hel is the plase for it.

Akordin tu skripter thar will be just about as many Kammills in heavin as rich men.

When yu korte a widder, yu want tu du it with spurs on.

Larfin at yure own story, while yu are tellin on it, is a good dele like firing a gun oph thru the tuch hole.

A pet lam, alwus makes a kross ram.

A live harte sumtimes gits intu a ded body, so dus perls git intu jersa clams.

"Glory enuff for one da," attendin a nigger kamp meeting.

He who skorns to be inflooensed at tall by fashun is a wize fool.

I am prepaired tu say tu sevin ov the rich men out ov evry ten, makes the most ov yure money for it makes the most ov yu.

If i had a boy who didn't lie well enuff tu sute me, i wud set him tu tendin a retale dri good store.

Man was kreated a little lower than the angells and has bin gittin a little lower ever sinse.

The moste oneasy kreetur i ever perused, was a bob tale bull, in fli time.

When a feller gits a goin down hil, it dus seem as tho evry thing had bin greased for the okashun.

I hav known folks whose *calibre* was very small, but whose *bore* was very big.

The meanest man i ever nu was the one who stole a suggar whissel from a nigger baby tu sweeten a kup ov rye koffee with.

Pluk is a nise kompound ov pride, vanitee and vartue.

Robbers are like rane, tha fall on the just and the unjust.

We hate those who will not take our advise, and despise them who do.

XXIX.

A FU REMARKS.

Moral swashun consis in asking a man tu do what he aught tu do without askin, and then beggin hiz pardon if he refuses tu do it.

I hav finally kum tu the konklusion, that a good reliable sett ov bowels, iz wurth more tu a man, than enny quantity ov brains.

Musick hath charms tu soothe a savage; this may be so, but i wud rather tri a revolver on him fust.

It alwus seemed to me that a left handed fiddler must pla the tune backwards.

I hav often bin told that the best wa iz tu take a "Bull bi the horns," but i think in many instanzes i shud prefer the "tale holt."

The fust law ov natur iz tu steal ; the sekund law is tu hide, and the third iz tu — steal agin.

Poverta acts the same onta a man's branes, az exercise dus onto hiz boddy, gives an appetite.

I never could cee any use in making wooden gods mail and femail.

If the harte iz rite, the hed cant be very rong.

Tha tell me that femails are so skarse, in the far western country, that a grate menny married wimmin are alreddy engaged tu their sekund and third husbands.

N. B.   The above remarks are not intended to be personal.

XXX.

A LEKTURE TO MALE YOUNG MEN ONLY.

Yu are about 2 begin life, yung men, for the fust time, and I suppose thare wud be no impropriety in mi saing, for the last time tew. It is hily important or thereabouts, that yu set down in sum kool plase, and take an honest akount ov stok, or in other wurds, less poetick but equally tru, yu sarch out the ramifikashun ov natur, and see what natur haz ramified yu for. Now skriptur will tell yu, that men don't gether pigs from thissels, neither dus the husband, nor hiz wife, nor euny ov his relashuns, plant korn when tha are after pumpkins, nor sow bukwheat, when he iz a lookin for old rye. Kauze and affeck iz anuther awful good thing to studdy; yu will find this talked ov in Dan Webster's dicktionary. Having follered the above advise, and having hefted the above reasoning, yu will cum tew the konklusion, whether it iz best for yu tu studdy law, or studdy shumaking, both ov them honerabil biznisses, and equally kondusiv tew helth. Yu will also be enabled tew bet with dispatch, whether yu hav a kall, tew preach the gospil, or sel yankee noshuns at auction, both ov them respektuous, if honestla follared, and both ov them liabel tew be led estra, and end at laste in the bronkeetis. The studdy ov medisin will present itself and flap its wings and crow, but it kant fule yu, bekause yu have sot down, as rekomended above, and tuk akount ov yure liabilitys, and kno tew a spot whether yu air konstructed rite for a veteran surgeon amung hosses, or hav the rite natur for dealing out kalamil & gallup amung men, wimmin & childrin. Yu will likewize hav it in yure power tew gess clussly between being a kolporter or keeping a billiard tabil; if yu find that yure goose iz morally sound, yu will itinerate at onst, but if yu diskiver a leak in yure base, yu will take up yure cue, naturally & akordinly. Selling dri goods and blaksmithing wil klaim yure especial notis, and wil bother yu dredfully for a verdik; but if yu find yu hav kalico on the brain, & aint afraid tew stretch the cloth & the truth a little, when yu mezure it, yu will straddle the kounter like an ingyrubber clothes pin, and smile on yure kustomers like a sleeping babe trubbled with wind. Yu wil, without doubt, be asked tu sa whether yu wil be a pollytisian or a blakleg, both equally honorabil. If yu hav enny reasonable douts about cheatin yure moste intimate frends, and aint willing tew be seen in low grogerys on lecktion daze, buying votes with cheap whiska and kounterfit munny, and dont expek tew buy yure elekshun, and then sell yure prinsiples tew git even; if yu kant.go this, and tend awl the churches near yu in rotashun, and hear folks sa, "What an ornyment to sosiety he iz!" i sa, if yu kant go all this without blushing, yu will ov course adopt the blakleg, and gain an honest living bi cheatin on the square.

Yung men yu will awl detek in this lekture a frendla feeling towards yu bi the author, and if yu foller the direckshuns laid down above, yu wil diskiver the wigglings ov yure genius, in time perhaps, tew saive yureselfs from cuming the govenor ov sum state, when natur kindly ramified yu for a carpenter and jiner.

XXXI.

CLEVER FELLOWS.

It is perfectly astounding how full ov *clever fellows* the world iz. Yu kan find them almost ennywhere, on the korner ov the streets, reddy tew say, "mi dear fellow how are yu?" and adjourn at onst tew the hotell and take a drink with yu. Yu can find them in the churches, reddy tew slap yu on the back and take yure meazure for a front pew, next tew the Hon. Hannibal Herring Hallibut, Esq., at the lucid figger ov $450 Dollars per year, and a liberal chanse at the contribushun plate, twice evry Sunda. Yu kan find them in the lucky possession ov a blood bay pair ov geldings sired by Casshus M. Klay, and jist refused tu the widder ov a defunk sope biler, at $2700 dollars, but tew yu! confidensially! tew yu!! tha will be placed at $2000. Yu kan find them in nominashun for congress, bland, fond, and peculiar, kneeling tew acksep yure sufrage as limber az a lover, ov the milk weed genus, at the balmorell ov a $30,000 Dollars maiden.— Yu can find them reddy tew indorse yure paper, *yesterday*, for awl the munny in the institushun. Good Lord! Good Lord! how thick tha are. I alwus treat theze fellers kindly, jist az tho i loved them, but i alwus stand in frunt ov them, az i do when i admire a mule. I dont think tha hav az mutch malis az impudense, and snm ov them are so innersent, that i really beleaf tha think tha are honest. I dont think the wurld could git along without theze clever feller, tha ar jist what keep truth above par, and furnish the romanse ov life with a continual freshness. I sa, long live theze clever fellers! and when tha die, if tha kan manage tew wiggle themselves into the better land, i am the last man who will desire to step on their tales.

XXXII.

AFFERISIMS.

God save the phools! and don't let them run out, for if it want for them, wise men couldn't get a livin.

Sum peoples branes are located in their heds.

We are told "that there want ennything maid in vain," but i hav thought that awl the time spent in manufakturing striped snaix, and muskeeters, waz wasted.

If thare waz nothing but truth in this wurld, a fool would stand just as good a chanse az a wize man.

True perlitenes consists in being anxus about the welfair ov uthers; false perliteness consists in being verry anxus about nothing.

Robbers are like rain, tha fall on the just, and the unjust.

If a man iz az wize az a sarpent, he can afford to be as harmless as a dove.

We are ap tu hate them, who wont take our advise, and despize them who do.

It iz dredful eazy tew be a phool — a man kan be one and not know it.

Real happiness dont consiss so mutch in what a man dont hav, az it duz, in what he dont want.

Fear iz the fust lesson larnt, and the laste one forgotten.

Noboddy but a phool, gits bit twise bi the samo dog.

XXXIII.

ANSWERS TO CONTRIBUTORS.

Josh Billings wants it respekfully understood, that, tho hiz duta az sensor ov a vartuous press ockasionally kauses him tew lite onto sum contributors at a high rate ov speed, he dus it, not out ov malis tu those who rite, but thru grate luv and tribulashun for thoze who read:

TO CONTRIBUTORS.

"*I Hear an Angell Whispre*," *by Clemantha.*— Theze lines contain more poeckry, and less truth. The fact is, Angells don't whispre, if tha hav got enny thing tew sa, tha sa it rite out loud. Tri agin, Clemantha; rite onto kontentment, or happiness, or sum sich subjec, that haint never bin rit onto.

"*Slavery, ordained ov God,*" *bi A. D. P.*— This produckshion we cant accept. We are bound in our insuranse polisy not tew hav on hand " enny article extra hazardus on akount ov fire," and we don't want tu be struk bi litenin, nor sent tu purgatory, and looze our insurance besides. Furthermore, writers must giv us their names in full; A. D. P. mite stand for *A. D—m Phule,* and we aint a doing enny bizness with them kind not if we are credibly informed.

' *On Pisgers nobil hites i stood, communin with our ansesters,*" *bi Clarense.*—Blank varse, bi grashus! If my memry dont fule me, this iz the same spot whare Noer stood, with the Ark previously. We aint mutch on blank varse, but think we smel a rat. We hav sent the peace tew the " Kommitty on forrin relashuns," and if tha sa the peace iz on the square, it will be published, ackompanied with a full sized 3 dollar puff.

"*Epitaff on a friend,*" *bi Emeline Parsons.*— Epitaffs are played out with us. We continu tew publish them, at 25 cents ahed, az we du deth and weddings, and dont hold ourself resposible for truth or damage. We luv tu enkurage genius tho, and advise Emeline Parsons tu diet, and keep her hand in bi riteing for the Nu York Leger.

"*Essa on Hurrykanes,*" *bi Tempest Jun'.*— Wil appear jist az soon az the hurrykane softens down a little. This writer handles a hurrykane the best we ever see it did. Hiz deskripshun resembles chain litening quietly. He maiks the grate oaks tew wiggle lik mad sarpents, and the roks tew bile and bust open, and the hole arth tew rumbil az tho it had the kolick. This writer could git up a ghost that would be wurth having. Tempest Jun' will pleze send us his photergraff, we want a personal intervu.

John Billings drives out to the Races.—See page 100.

XXXIV.

A SHORT AND VERY AFFEKTING ESSA ON MAN.

Man iz a problem not yet solved, made out ov dirt, and smells ov the material. He waz kreated a little lower than the angells, and haz bin gittin a little lower ever sinse. He waz given a butiful hum, clus tew the borders ov heaven, the fruit and the flower waz planted for him, and the sweet waters were led along hiz futpath, birds sung onla for him, and woman was bilt tew make hiz joy komplete. The lam laid her hed on the lion's buzzum, and the viper knu not ov his sting. The winds waz tempered with soft fragranse, and awl things had onla the soul ov innersence in them. Guile there waz none, fear there waz none, even hope thare waz none, for thare waz nothing tew want. This waz butiful tew behold, but it didn't prove enny thing, but the kindness ov God. Could the arth be peopled? could the oseans be crossed? could the forest be chopped down? could sittys be built? could enny boddy be made tew work when thare waz nothing to hope for and nothing tew want? Man waz created tew govern a world ov ruggidness, and he couldn't dew it bi being as harmless as a dove; he must hav a touch ov a good sized sarpent in him, or he would hav lived, he and hiz wife, growing butiful and useless, forever, in the Garden ov Eden. Man never waz bilt for the Garden ov Eden; he waz onla put thare tew see its buty, but not tew enjoy it till he had arnt it; not tew liv thare untill a weary round had bin paced. Eden waz hiz kradle, Eden was the pla ground ov hiz yung Adamhood, and under hiz vine and fig treeze waz hiz old age tew be gathered. How menny ov the countless millions, who hav gone forth from the pearly gate ov the garden hav ever entered agin? Sum few, perhaps hav got back, weary and worn, sum few hav got back within sight ov its glory, and sleep thare, but legions lay whare they hav fell az far from their hum az wandering feet could carry them; and man after 5,000 years ov birthrite tew awl the glora ov heaven, and arth, iz az mutch ov a problem az ever. If he governs the arth — if the lightnings obey him — if art iz the monark ov natur, and if even the angels are at times tempted tew admire him, strugling with the sarpent, iz he not, at this day, a moste magnificent failure? kan he, who haz governed so mutch, that even angels would shudder tew attack, can he govern *himself*. This iz the problem. It iz but a step from the furtherest grave tew the garden ov Eden, but how few will take it. We awl know the wa back tew the kradle ov Eden. We awl long tew be thare asleep, but if God dont take us in hiz arms, az froward children are taken, how few thare will be, who will ever git hum. Man iz the problem, God iz the solution.

XXXV.

THE RASE KOARSE.

"Grate rase! at Sulphur Flat trotting Park, on Thursda, April 9th, for a puss ov 13 dollars, and a bulls-eye watch, free for awl hosses, mares, geldings, mules, and Jackasses!"

Seeing the above anounsement, pasted up on a gide board, at "Jamaka rum four corners," and having never saw a hoss trot, on a well regulated rase koarse, for the improvement ov the breed ov hosses, i agreed i wud go, jist tew encourage the breeding ov good hosses. I found the village of Sulphur Flats located in a lot and well watered bi a griss-mill and 2 tannerys. The prinsipal buildings seem tu consiss ov a tavern stand, 3 groserys, an insurance offiss, and anuther tavern stand, awl condukted on strik whiskee prinsiples. I found the inhabitants a good deal tired in their religus views, and i thought the opening wud admit 3 or 4 missionarys abreast.

The moste prinsipal bizness ov the peopil waz pealing bark in the winter, and pitchin cents az soon az warm wether sot in. I asked a gentleman present, who ced he waz a reporter for "The Yung Man's Christian Gide," if he knew what the poplashun ov the plase definitely waz, and he ced he definitely didn't, but if i would set out a pail ov whiskee, with a dipper into it, on the top ov a hemlock stump, that grew in front ov the tavern, it wouldn't be 60 minnits befour i cud count the whole ov them, and then we both ov us smiled, az it were, tew onst. Having asked sum uther inquirys, ov a mexed natur, i santered down tu where the rase koarse waz.

THE TRACK.

I found the track waz about a mild in circumferense, and ov a sandy disposishun, fensed in by a kranbury mash on one side, and a brush fense on tuther, and in jist about 3 minnet condishun. The judge's stand waz an ox cart surrounded on the sides bi a ba rigging, and the reporters waz invited tew git intu the cart.

THE HOSSES

Waz a gra mare, about the usual stature, not verry fat, and laboring under a spring halt, which tha ced she had caught ov anuther hoss, about 10 days ago. Tha ced she had trotted tu a kamp-meeting last fall inside ov a verry short time, and that her back bone waz awl game. I asked a yung man with long yeller hair and bedtick pantyloons on, who waz currying oph the mare, what her pedigree was, and he with a wink tew anuther feller who stood clus bi, ced, "she waz got bi the Landlord out ov a Methdiss minister," and then tha both laffed. I found out bi inquirin, that her name waz "Fryin-Pan." The uther hoss waz a red hoss, rather hastily konstructed, with a spare tale on him, which tha ced waz kaused by his trotting so fast, in a windy day ; i shud think he waz about 5 feet and a haf in hite, and ov a kickin natur. Tha ced he waz a stranger in theze parts, and that his rite name waz "Juise Harp."

FUST HEAT.

The hosses both cum up tew tho skore in the immejiate visinity ov each uther, and got the wurd tew go, the fust time. The gra mare waz druv bi "Dave Larkin," and the hoss was handled bi "Ligh Turner." Tha trotted sublimely, az clus az the Siamese twins; the mare with her hed hi up and her noze full ov winde; the hoss waz stretched out tite, like a chalk line; tha passed the haf mile pole simultaneously, time, 2 minnits. Now the kontest becum exsiting, "Dave" hollered, and "Ligh" yelled — on tha kum, the mare gru higher, and the hoss gru longer — tha make the last turn tew onst — tha look like a dubble team — the exsitement grows more intensely — the crowd sways to and fro — the ox cart trembles — tha cum! tha cum! sich shouting, sich yelling, sich swearing, sich chawing terbacker, waz never herd before; the mare iz ahed! — no, the hoss iz ahed! 'tis even, 'tis a ded hete, tha pass the ox-kart — the hoss wins hi 3 quarters ov an inch, time 4 minnits lacking 2 seckunds.

REMARKS.

The hosses ar surrounded bi a crowd ov men, wimmin, and children. Each party are sanguinary ov suckces. The bettin iz 2 quarts ov whiskee to anything, on the red hoss. At this junkture the gentleman, reporter for the Young Man's Christian Gide, propozed tew bet 75 cents that the mare wud win the nex heat; i tuk the proposishun forthwithly, and the steaks, bi mutual consent, was placed in mi hat and sot under the kart, and here let me stait, before i forget it, that i haint saw the steaks nor the hat sinse.

SECKUND HEAT.

The hosses both sho signs ov distress. The gra mare's ears hang down the side ov her hed, like two wet rags, and the hoss rests his tale on the ground. Tha go slola bak tew the distanse pole, and cum up agin tew the skore, az tho tha waz yoked together. Awa tha go; the hoss a leetle ahed. The hoss leads tew the haf mild pole in 2:30. On the bak stretch, "Dave" went at the mare with hiz long purswader; she trots like litening, she passes the hoss! no! she busts! she busts! and befour "Dave" cud flatten her down tew her work, she broke from the trak and trotted clean up tew her hips in the krambery mash. The hoss cum in awl alone, trotting fast, and so clus down, that 2 feet ov his tale dragged on the ground. Time ov this heat, not fur from 5 minnits, "Juise Harp" winning, bi a quarter ov a mild. Thus ended the grate rase at "Sulphur Flats." I immejiately started on foot for "Jamaka Rum four corners," bare headed, but fully impressed that, tho men, and even whiskee mite deteryoate, the breed ov hosses must begin tew improve in that seckshun ov the kuntry in a fu dais.

XXXVI.

"GIV THE DEVIL HIZ DUE."

This z good advise. I don't kno who waz the auther ov it, if I did, i wud go for rewarding him, either with a sett ov plated ware, or a prize in the art union. No man kould giv better advise, or consolashun; he ought tew hav a 2 story monament, when he dize, with an epitaff on it, founded on fack; he ought tew hav at leaste fifteen hundred little children named after him each year; he ought tew be nussed in men's memorys like a plesant dreme, that afterwards turned out tew be true. He ought to hav his fotograph taken bi evry new sky-lite in the land, he ought tew be sett tew musick, and be sung in conneckshun with the docksaloger; he ought tew be stereotyped, so that nu edishuns could constantly be worked oph tew meet the pressing demand.

"Giv the Devil hiz due." Yung man, this advise was got up for yu. If yu owe the Devil ennything pay him off at onse, and then discharge him, and dont hire him over agin at enny prise. That's what the author ment. Be honest, pay even the devil, if yu owe him, but dont owe him agin. If the proprietor ov this most worthy proverb, "Giv the devil hiz due," still lives, altho i haint had the pleasure ov an introducksion tew him, if he ever wants enny thing, *even good advise*, he kan git it in awl natiff purity and innersense, bi dropping a line tu his everlasting well wisher.

JOSH BILLINGS.

XXXVII.

WATCH DOGS.

Mi dearly beloved christian friend, did yu ever visit enny body? Did yu ever visit enny boddy who resided in the subburbs? Did yu ever visit enny boddy who resided in the subburbs, and kept a grate lank, watery-eyed, yeller dog, with very long hare on hiz bak? — Did yu ever hav this grate lank, yeller-devil dog cum loping down tu the frunt gate, tu welcum yu with a hiena yowl, and with the long hare on hiz bak pitching forward az tho it wud cum out bi the rutes, and his tale awl swelled up like a settin hen's? Kan yu rekolek the horrid fear that seized upon yu, and froze yu fast tu the arth, az the monster foamed in rage around yu? Yu gaze in agny tords the hous — it seems 3 weeks at least. At last the frunt door kautiously opens — yure lady friend recognizes yu: "Bless me! Mrs. Bingler, how glad i am tew cee yu! dew cum rite in.

How pale the walk has made yu! Tiger! Tiger! hush yu! He is onla glad tew cee yu. Dew cum rite in, Mrs. Bingler." Mrs. Bingler, let me ask yu a question, privately: "Dew yu kandidly think that the luv yu bare for yure lady friend, Mrs. Baremore, who livs in the subberbs, iz enny kind ov atonement for the hate and horror that yu will alwus hav for the grate lank, watery-eyed, yeller dog Tiger that she keeps tew welcum her visitors with? If yu dew, please address, postage paid, JOSH BILLINGS, Box 467, Pokeepsie sitty.

XXXVIII.

ANSWER TO CONTRIBUTORS.

Amerikus.—Your contribushun is in hand. We like its fluidness. It is like ile on a side hill. Natur haz did a good thing for yu, and yu ought tew be willing tew dew a good thing for natur. This line in your produkshun strikes us as very butiful and original; "And larn the luxury of dewing good." Gold smith hisself mite hav bin proud ov sich a line. And again; "Oh would sum power the gifty giv us, ov seeing oursels as uthers cee us;" yure idee ov indroducing the skotch acksent into yure stile, is verry happee. If yu never hav red Robert Burns, yu will be suprised to larn that his style verry mutch resembles yures. Onse more yu sa; "If ignoranse is bliss, tis folly tew be wise." This sentiment is jist as tru as tis common. Pope, I think, has sumthing similar; but awl grate minds sometimes express theirselfs alike. Yure contribushun will appear in our nex issu, with a *wood cut* piktur ov a saw buck at the top ov it.

Beta—I think sumly as yu do, "this wurld is all a fleetin cirkus, for man's illushun given," but that aint no rezon for not pitching in and being illusioned onse in a while. I wouldn't giv a cent for a man who hadn't bin illusioned, and who didn't expect tew be several times agin.

Mathew.—I see bi yure letter that yu hav determined tew studdy ministry. Yu sa yu hav doubts about yure talents being enuffly tew make a minister; i don't think that ought tew bluff yu oph, for i hav saw menny men ov almity mean tallents, who got tew be first rate ministers.

Philander.—Yu ask me which iz the most best, the marrid or the single condishun?—Most evry boddy, at sum time in their life, has tried the single state; also, moste evry boddy haz hankered after the double state, or married condishun. I hav tried both states, and am reddy to sware, that if a man kan git a woman who kan fri pancakes on both sides without burning them, and dont hanker tew be a wimmin's kommitty, the marrid state iz a heaven and arth, awl tew onst. But after awl the married state is a good deal like falling out ov a cherry tree, if a person don't happen tew git hurt, it is a good reason for not trieing it agin.

XXXIX.

REMARKS.

It is highly important, when a man makes up his minde tew bekum a raskall, that he shud examine hisself clusly, and see if he aint better konstructed for a phool.

I argy in this way, if a man is right he cant be too radikal, if he is rong he kant be too conservatiff.

"Tell the truth, and shame the Devil;" i kno lots ov people, who can shame the devil easy enuff but the tother thing bothers them.

If yu don't beleaf in "total depravity," buy a quart ov gin and studdy it.

Their is one advantage in a plurality ov wifes; tha fite each other, insted ov their hustbands.

It is a verry delicate job to forgive a man, without lowering him in his own estimashun, and yures too.

As a gineral thing, when a woman wares the britches, she has a good rite tew them.

I am poor, and I am glad that i am, for i find that wealth makes more people mean, than it duz generous.

Woman's inflooense is powerful — espeshila when she wants enny thing.

No man luvs tu git beat, but it is better tew git beat than tew be rong.

Awl kind ov bores are a nuisance, but it is better tew be bored with a 2 inch auger, than a gimblet.

"Be sure yu are rite then go ahed;" but in kase ov doubt go ahed enny wa.

Sekts and creeds ov religion, are like pocket compesses, good enuff tu pinte out the direction, but the nearer the pole yu git the wuss tha wurk.

The rode tew Ruin, is alwus kept in good repair, and the travellers pay the expense ov it.

If a man begins life bi being fust Lutenant in his familee, he never need to look for promoshun.

I hav got as much munny as sum folks, but i hav got as much impudence as enny ov them, and that is the next thing tew munny.

It aint often that a man's reputashun outlasts his munny.

Dont mistake arroganse for wisdum; menny people hav thought tha was wise, when tha was onla windy.

The man who kant git ahed, without pulling others back, iz a limited cuss.

Woman will sumtimes confess her sins, but i never knu one tu confess her faults.

Thare is onla one advantage, that i kan see, in going tew the Devil, and that is, the rode is easy, and yu are sure tew git thare.

Lastly — i am violently opposed tu arden spee-rits as a bevridge, but for manufaktering purposes, i think a leetle of it tastes good.

XL.

AN ESSA ONTO MUSIK.

"Musick hath charms to sooth a savage.
To rend a rok or split a kabbage."

So tha tell me, but i shud rather try a revolver on the savage, a blast ov powder on the rok, and good sharp vinegar on the kabbage. I haint searched history tew diskiver who giv the first consert ov musik. We are told, that in *those days* "the stars sang together," but in *theze days* yu kant git stars tew sing together. We often hear it said, "that such a person haz a good ear for musik." I don't fellership this remark; awl a person wants tew understand musik with, is a good soul; a "good ear" haint got enny more tew du with it than a good sett ov brains has tu do with charity. Musical crickets insist that if the gammut aint rite, the musik aint rite; this is awl nonsense; the gammut haint got enny more tew du with a musick-hungry man, than a knife and fork has with his dinner, if he is real hungry he can eat with his fingers. Musick want got up tew make us wise, but better natured. How much opera musick dew you suppose it wud taik tu make a man cry? Folks will tell yu that such an "overture fria dabulo" (or sum uther furrin big named thing) "waz moste heavenly rendered," tha mite as well tell me that a pumpkin pie was heavenly rendered. What do i care about the rendering, if i don't git a piece ov the pie? Let some Prime Donner, or Mezzer Soapraner, or Barrytown Base, or some sich latin individual, cum into this village, and histe their flag, and hav a programmy ov singing as long as a sarch warrant, and as hard tu spell out as a chinese proklamashun ritten upside down, and taxed seventy-five cents for a preserved seat, and moste evrybody will go tu hear it, bekause moste everybody else dus, and will sa. evry now and then, (out loud) "how bewitching! how delishus! how egstatick!" and nineteen out ov evry twenty-one ov them wouldn't kno it if the performance was a burlesk on their grandmother. Wouldn't it be fun tew cee one ov these opera singers undertake tu rok a baby tu sleep? i gess thare wud be two parts carried tu that song about that time. Suppoze yu shud come home at nite, a weary boy, and la yure hed in mother's lap, and she shud let out a opera, good Lord! wouldn't yu think yure mother was a lunatik, or ought to be one at onst, tu save her karacter. "Korrect taist," iz anuther big wurd; ive herd folks uze it whose finger nales wanted cleaning. Musik, after all, is sumthing like vittels, the more cooking and seasoning we uze, the more we have to hav, till after awhile we kant enjoy ennything ov the vittels but the pepper.— Opera dont hav enny more loosening affeck on me, than caster ile wud on a graven image. I set and gaze, and hark, and cee the whole aujence in hiroglipbicks, and awl i kan do iz tu git mad that sich stuff is called musik. But awl the reasoning in the wurld wont convince menny people that tha haint got a rite tew go into fits over an opera tha dont understand a word ov; it iz the fashion tew expire and hav their souls dissolve in latin at the rate ov seventy-five cents, an it haz got to be did, "sink or swim, survive or perish." If enny boddy wants tu go and hear a man or woman disgorge musik, that has more kolik than melody into it, i suppose (under the constitushun) tha hav jist the same rite tew crusifi themselves enny uther wa, for sumbody's else sins that tha dont kno the natur of.

XLI.

"MAN WAZ MADE TEW MOURN."

This waz the private opinion ov one Burns, a Skotchman, who waz very edikated tew poetri from his infansy. I and he differ, which is not uncommon among grate minds. The ornary minds in this wurld are disposed tew coinside, which iz the reson whi superstitions prevale so mutch. Tew differ upon matters with anuther is a fair presumpshun that yu are in the habit ov smelling ov things before yu swaller them. Man warnt made tew mourn, man waz made tew laff. He iz the onla creeter or thing that God made tew laff out loud. It iz tru he knows how to mourn, so duz the animills kno how, the birds can tell their sorrows, and the flowers kan hang their pretty heds. Man waz made tew smile, tew laff, tew haw! tew thro up his hat, and sing halleluger. Man waz made tew praze God, and he cant dew it hi mourning. Awl the mourning thare

Josh Billings wants to kuow why it is that so many women who are so thin in the face, stick out so everywhere else.—*See page* 122.

iz in this wurld was introduced bi man; man warnt made tew mourn any more than he was made to crawl. Tharfore i sa tew awl men and women, stop crying and go tew laffing, yu will last longer, and git fatter and stand jist as good a chanse tew git tew heaven with a smile on your countenansc, as yu will with yure fase leaking at every pore. I sa man want made tew mourn, if he had bin he would not hav bin put in Paradise, whare every thing else was made in the image ov smiles.

P. S.—I don't want ennybody tew think that i am down on Burns, for i dew consider him the most Poet that ever lived. I had ruther be the authur ov one poum i kno ov, that he rit, than tew be king and queen ov England, and keep a hoss and carriage; but "man warnt made tew mourn" Robert Burns, he iz the kause of his own sorrow. For enny further informashun tutching this subjek, address, post paid, with stamp enclosed.

JOSH BILLINGS.

XLII.

PROVERBS.

What a sarkasm it is tew a ded man's memory, tew ask "how much munny he left?"

I don't like tew be alwus a asking questions, but i would really like tu kno whi it is that so manny wimmin who are so thin in the face, stick out so every where else!

Tha tell ov an orful sharp feller out west, who broke out ov an alms houze and made sixteen hundred and thirty two $\frac{75}{100}$ dollars, in the substitude bizness, before tha kould ketch him.

The bible asks us, "what will it proffitt a man, if he gain the whole world and loze hiz own soul?" i suppose this depends sumwhat upon the size ov the soul, i think thare are kases whare the trade would do.

The term "skunked," which we often hear applied tew them that gits beat, waz diskovered in this wa: a Radikal and a Conservatiff, went out hunting skunks. The Radikal diskovered one at sum distanse off and without trieing tew git nearer, drew up his musquet, and shot him ded. The Consarvatiff undertook tew ketch his skunk alive, and the konsequents waz, he got — skunked.

The old proverb sez, " Giv the Devil his due!" if this is put thru, what will bekum ov yu, mi friend? and the rest ov the — nabors?

XLIII.

KISSING CONSIDERED.

"Man was made tew mourn," so warbled Burns, "and woman was made tew kiss," so warbles Billings. One ov these centiments haz bin alreddy immortalised, and the other i intend shall be as soon as the Legislater meets. I am not yet lusid how i shall bring the matter befoar that honorabil boddy; but i dew kno how the honorabel boddy feals on the subject, and how tha will act if ever tha hav a good chanse. To give a fertile and golden opinyun, upon kissing in the lump, and kissing in the detale, requires a man ov truth, and sum experiense in tasteing.

IN THE LUMP.

Kissing iz one ov those fu things that is easier dun than deskribed; in fack, about the onla way tew deskribe it well is tew do it well. It iz, without doubt, a verry anshunt enterprise; and judgeing from what we kno ov human natur in this latitude, it must hav struk Adam as a good investment when he fust diskovered hiz wife. If Adam didn't kiss Eve at sight he aint the man i take him tew be; and if Eve didn't relish it, it must hav bin bekause it want well did. Thare iz one thing about kissing in the lump, diffrent from the rest ov the fine arts and that iz, it don't require enny eddikashun tew dew it; i hav even thort that the more unedikated it waz did (provided it didn't miss the mark) the more touching it was tew behold. But kissing is a good deal like eating; thare is not much fun (when a person iz hungry) in standing by, and see it did bi anuther fellow, if it iz did ever so well. It is one ov the cheapess and healthyess luxurys ov the season, and don't sho enny disposishun tew go out ov fashion, and will keep sweet in enny climate. Upon the whole, if yu examine kissing in the lump, clussly, yu will be led tew exclaim: Fustly, that it iz as easy tew hav it did, az it is handy tew dew it. Sekundly, that it is like Cowpers tea, it cures a man without corning him; and, Thirdly, it is a frugal, highly consentrated, and reverend luxury.

IN DETALE.

When we cum tew thro oph glittering generalitys and approach our subjeck in single file, it is then that the divinitee ov the art seems to be spotted; and reveals tew us awl the shades ov pomp and sirkumstanze, from the sublime and tender, clear down tew the redikilus and tuff. Mother's kiss and little baby's kiss are az pure az the utterance ov angells; so is the artless kiss ov sister Mary and — couzin Fanny; but thare iz one cold, blu, lean kiss, that alwus makes me shiver tew see. Two persons (ov the femail perswashun) who hav witnesst a grate menny younger and more pulpy daze, meet in sum publik plase, and not having saw each uther for 24 hours tha kiss immegiately; then tha talk about the weather, and the young man who preached yesterday, and then tha kiss immegiately, and then tha blush and laff at what tha sa tew each other, and kiss agin immegiately. I would not objeckt tew awl this if it want sich a waste ov swetness on the dessart air. I am willing tew be sworn that this kind ov kissing alwus puts me in minde ov two olde flints trieing tew strike fire. How different this from the konnubial kiss i witnesst laste nite. I knu he wast a husband jist got back from a bizzness tower, bi hiz haste. He passt me at the korner below, and awl unexpected enkountered hiz wife, and as natral as the bee tew the the flower, tha flu together. Thare want enny thing sentimental about that kiss; thare want enny thing criminal about it. It rang out on the air as clear as the challenge ov a perlice offiser — it filled a whole block. Thare want mutch prelimnary about it neither, for it smashed a 50 dollar bonnett, and muxed up a barricade ov edging and frizzled tucker. It want the fust one, it waz tew well did for that. It want the sipping ov two trembling lovers, afraid ov the echo; it want studdyed out nor stolen, but it wast full ov honest ripeness and chastened struggle which made me hanker for — for, one oph from the same peace. Jist one more remark and I am thru. Thare is one kind ov kissing that has alwus been deeemd extra hazardous (on akount ov fire) and that is kissing yure naber's wife. Gitting the wife's consent don't seem tew make the matter enny the less risky.

MORAL.—Don't eat onions during the kissing seazon unless yu chew them well.

XLIV.

FOR A FU MINNITS AMUNG THE SPEERITS.

Bi invitashun i had the happiness tew attend a speerit cirkle in the good old town ov Billingsville last week. A long haired feller bi the name of Professer McGuire, with a face that looked like a sucked lemon, waz the midwife ov the okasion. It seemed that a Mister Bloodgood wanted a dispatch from Miss Jerusha Perkins, who, he claimed, was in the speerit land. After the kandel waz subdued and strikt silence ensued, sum ov the alfiredest thumps took plase on the tabel; mi hair begin tew stan up, and i wished i waz out ov the consarn; but after taking an akount ov stock i cum tew the inference that i could knock the spots oph from the whole bileing ov them, if it cum to actooal bizzness i agreed tew set still and see the whole sport.

In a fu space ov time McGuire begin tew git news

from Jerusha, which he ced waz official and waz in the shape ov a letter, and he wud translate it as follers:

May 20th, SPEERIT LAND, 1846.

"*Dear Augustus Sidney Bloodgood:* Having a fu spare time tew devote terestial things, i take mi pen in hand tew rite yu a fu lines. I am well, and hope theze fu lines will find yu enjoying the same blessin. I hav jist returned from the gardin ov Eden whare i hav bin with Dave Sturgiss, who was killed at the battell ov Gettisburg bi gitting choked with a pease ov hard tacks. The weather iz fine, and there iz evry prospeck ov krops; I never see the potaters look finer. Dri goods is cheap here, yu can buy good factory cottin cloth, yard wide, for eleven cents a yard and hav thred thrown in. I see the Widder Bostwick yesterday, she looks as starched up as ever.

"Would yu beleaf it, dear Augustus, that ugly Miss Snubdin is here, how yu used tew hate her! yu kno yu used tew sa that she wud go tew that uther land ov speerits. Let me hear from yu oftin thru the dear McGuire. Me and anuther speerit bi the name of Julia roost on the same celestial tree, and we oftin talk over the fellers we used tu know, and yu kan bet high, dear Augustus, that yu are the one that i brag on. Don't let enny ov them terestial mortals fool yu with their luv, for Jerusha's essence has no affinitee but for her corporeal jewell, Augustus Sidney Bloodgood."

At this junkter thare waz 6 raps on the tabel about az fast and loud az tho there waz playing kards, and sumboddy about being eukered; then awl was still and the kandels waz lit, and evry boddy sot in aw and amazement. The sircle broke up immejiately, and i passed out with mi frend, who asked me what i thought ov speerit manifestashuns now. I told him i thought if evrything waz on the square, that Bloodgood had a ded sure thing on Jerush.

XLV.

SAYINGS.

A gest is sumthin that is sharp enuff to be notised, and not rude enuff tu be resented.

"Solaman was a wize man," but when he ced thar warnt enny thing nu under the sun, he hadn't herd ov Hudsin River time tables.

"Large bodys move slo," this ere proverb dont apply tu lies, for the bigger tha ar, the faster tha go.

The only wa tu pleze evra boddy, is tu make evry boddy think yu ar a bigger fule than tha ar.

Ignorance is ced tu be bliss, this ma be so, I never tried it.

It's just as natral for lawyers tu lie, as it is for a white hared yung one's nose tu run.

The man who kan ware a shirt a hole week, and keap, it klean, aint fit for enny thing else.

The more we hav, the more we want, and the more we want, the less we hav.

"The law ov nashuns;" iron klad gun botes.

Evra sorrow has its twin joy; the fun of skraching almost pays for having the ich.

XLVI.

JOSH GOES TO LONG BRANCH.

"Hum agin! Hum agin! from a forrin shore!" or in uther wurds less juicy but equally tru, i hav got back from Long Branche, whither i went tew git mi buty and health restored. I waz thare 2 weeks, and lost 50 pounds in munny, and gained 10 pounds in meat. i feal like a fur tippet. I shall go down nex summer, if mi life iz spared also. I made a grate menny nu ackquaintance, that will be hard tew fergit, amung which, waz a nu kind of likker, which they kall apple toddy; this likker would be an invaluable dockument tew take amung the heathen tew convert them; 2 horns ov it would set them crazy — for civilizashun. The natur ov the sile or land there iz impregnated with sand, which iz adapted tew raisin a dust when the wind bloze, and also iz capabel ov produsing, (az i see bi the statisticks ov the state sensus) more fleas tew the aker without the aid ov manure, than iz needed for hum consumption. The two prinsipal attrackshuns thero iz the air, and the water, which are to be had in enny quantity, at a slite advanse from fust cost. The men and wimmin go in swimming together which at the fust sight looks a leetle risky, but az soon az they git used tew it, tha tell me, tha aint afrade ov each other at all. Thare iz 15 taverns at Long Branch, and thare iz ground room tew build more ov them, and az far az i kno, no man need tew go away without spending awl ov hiz munny, if he haz got enny ambishun about him. Thare waz sevral verry fashionable wimmin on exhibishun thare, and altho they didn't hav on mutch clothes, what they did hav, waz wuth the munny. I also saw sevral diamonds thare, which they ced were discovered at little falls, in this state, and waz wuth respectfully, from 2, to 5 dollars. One verry pleazing feeter waz the fast trotting hosses which belonged tew the natives ov the surrounding country, which were brought down in front ov the taverns evry day, tew trot for the amuzement, & instruktion, ov the guests. The Hosses didn't seem to me tew trot az fast az the drivers did, but i dont think enny body ever saw more dust raized, still, if hollering out loud iz enny sign that the hosses waz a trotting fast, then Flory Temple never had any bizness at Long Branch, unless it waz for her health. Hoss trotting iz at best a cruel enterprize, but when it iz gone into, with slow hosses, and unskillful drivers, it iz about az disgusting az the opening ov Rockaway clams, with a shoe-hammer. You will find awl the different styles ov docktrine and pollyticks, at Long Branche. One feller asked me "if i didn't think that the southern confederasy would be recognized before long," and i ced, that the southren confederasy had bin *recognized*, for more than 3 years, bi awl sensibel & honest people, az the moste cussidest ov awl things cussid. And another feller asked me what i thought ov the doktrine ov poligamy. i replied tew him, in a few wurds, that it waz tew mutch doktrine, for enny one man tew hav, and dew the subjeck justiss. Az good a way az enny tew git tew Long Branch, iz bi the steam Bote Jesser Hoyt, and the Delaware Ba ralerode. The cars on this rale rode will put enny man in minde ov one ov the cages in which van amburgh's trained animels are carried around the kuntry, and az for speed, thare iz but one thing on arth slower, and that iz a bread pill. In konclusion, Long Branch iz about the onla thing in the state ov Nu Jersee, that dont belong tew the Camptown, and Amboy Ralerode, and ought tew be visited as a natral curiosity on that vera akount, if for no uther. The prinsipel amuzements ov the plase are pitching cents, and walking a mile and a half, back into the kuntry, tew see a liberty pole, Thare iz one custom thare that mite be altered, if it couldn't be improved, and that iz awl the niggers seem tew hav bin born for the express purpiss ov standing around when a guest leaves, with evry feature in their fase resembling a 25 cent shinplaster in distress, and even the Landlord's look, and act az tho you waz going oph, without paying them awl the munny yu had. Visiting Long Branch, in this respeck, iz like going down into a marsh, in muskeeter time, awl the inhabitants stick a bill into you. Thare iz no ingenuity in this wa ov skinning a man, it iz like skinning a cat, a little evry day, tew make it hurt less.

     Yours at sight, Josh Billings.

XLVII.

TO MY LADY CORRESPONDENTS.

Cora.—Now yu ask me tew mutch. I kant giv no sartin resippee tew make a feller pop the question. Sum men are awful slow on a court, tha are like olde houn dogs, all tha want iz to be sure tha are on the rite track, and don't seem tew kare if tha don't never cum up with the game. If i was a gal, and one ov this kind ov dogs got after me, i wud hole rite off, and if he didn't commense tu dig me out at onst, i shud kno he waz only hunting for fun.

Rebekar.— I am dredful sorry tew hear yu are a widder. I kno how tu pity yu, i haint never bin a widder miself, but i hav bin in a habit ov pittying widders, for a grate length ov time. And yu tell me yu are a yung widder too, wuss and wusser. If yu find that thare aint nobody in yure naberhood who understands pittying yung widders, let me kno at onst, and i will see what kan be did for yu.

Flora.— I like yure spirit, yu hav got a soul. Thare aint no diskount on to it. Stan yure ground, don't giv an inch, the olde man will cum to hiz milk bimeby. The idee that yu kant hav a bonnet az good as Sal Parker haz got, iz darned likely. If i waz a gal, and mi olde man wouldn't go 50 dollars for me a plane bonnet, blame me if i wouldn't go into a dekline, spit blood, or hav a pane in the bak, or see a ghost, and set and shiver till the olde man cum doun with the bonnet.

Lizzy.— Yu sa yu are sixteen years old, and aint marrid yet. That looks a little dusty, but don't dispare, az long az thare iz life theres hope. If i hear ov enny boddy looking around for a woman, ill let yu kno forthwithly. Send me forty or fifty ov yure fotograffs, tha are good things tu skatter around luce. Az i ced in mi last letter i kant la doun no rule tu kech a hustband, men kant tell themselves half the time what ketched them, awl tha kno iz that tha git keched the cussedest evra now and then.

Matilda.— Lap dogs are verry skase jist now prinsipally owing tew the skasity ov them. I see one yesterda that was almost heavenly. The owner asked 50 dollars for him, he had sore eys, and the itch, but tha tell me that awl lap dogs haz theze trifling komplantes. I saw anuther one, which the owner onla asked thirty-five dollars for, he had small sized fits, but waz warrented not tew hav more than three fits in enny one da. I think this dog iz jist what yu are looking for; i offered thirty-seven dollars for him, if the owner wud heave in a vial ov fits medisin. He is tew giv me an anser tomorrow.

P. S.—I hav bought the dog and will send him bi xpress. hiz name iz Agusty Seazer.

XLVIII.

ON WIDDERS.

Widders are an interesting studdy. Tha ma be dividid (tew anser our purpis,) into 3 classes: *The Lone, The Grass,* and *The Star Spangled Banner Widder.* The Lone Widder iz ginerally selebrated for her piety, she haz passed the middle ov life, she knows she haz got gra hairs in her hed, she will tell her age, and talks tenderla ov her ded husband. Her grief iz sober, her weeds are rank, if she iz ritch, she is charitable, if she is poor, she is humble. She seldum marrys the sekund time. Her cheerfulness never bekums gayety, and her sorrow never bekums lamentashun. If she has children, she treats them as the partners ov her bereavment, if she has none, she bends down tew those she meets as she wud tew the arly flower in her pathway. Her hole life is a glora tew her sek, and an honour evra da tew him whose good memry amung men she perpetuates.

The Grass Widder is marrid without enny husband. She keeps house at a hotel, and kalls the servants bi familiar names. She sez that her husband is a kurnel in the armee. Her thesis is unkongenial tempraments, she kan repeat Don Juan, and hides Boccassio's tales under her pillow. If she wud ride out she orders a coach, and a gentleman; if she is ritch, she is arrogant, if she is poor, she is brasen. She kalls virtue prudery, and sez she wouldn't swop chastity with Dianner. If her kurnel is fortunate enuff tew git shot in battle, yu ma meet her and hiz Lutenant at Nuport nex summer, marrid — for the season.

The Star Spangled Widder iz yung, ornamental, and — a fule. She marrid her husband bekauze hiz name waz Alphonzo, and she mourns for him in at least 50 feet ov krape. Her fingers are as jewelled as the hilt ov a spanish dagger. She was eddikated at a fust klass seminare, with a 9 months' vakashun in it evry year, and talks awl the languages, excep english, bravely. She gases on you from beneath her limber eyelashes, as pensiv as a wel fed kitten. Yu ma think she wants tew marry, but she thinks she onla wants a frlend. If she shud snare some old feller, with a full puss, she wil make him a good toddy stik for his beverage. She has more chastity than sens, and more vartue than affeckshun.

Upon refleckshun i am disposed tew sa that there iz no condishun that a woman iz kalled upon tew fill so delikate, and so diffikult, as the widder; a condishun in which the lovlaness ov their naturs kan be made tew challenge our respek and admirashun, az alzo, a condishun in which their frailties may exsite our abhorrense, and their weakness, our disguss — Amen!

XLIX.

THINGS THAT I DON'T HANKER AFTER TO SEE.

A man out at the elbows, and his wife out tew a woman's rites convenshun.

A yung lady ov more circumference than the diameter ov her father's real estate.

A boy under 15 with over 15 bad habits.

A long bill at the tailor's, that belongs tew a short Bill at the St. Nicholas.

A man who haz more hair under his nose than knows under his hair.

A virgin who haz beat 40, afrade ov a rane *bo*.

A pollytision leading in prayer.

A man whoze houze wants painting a different culler from hiz noze.

Charitee that evra boddy knowz ov.

A house so divided agin itself, that it dont kno which wa tew fall.

"Augers that won't bore," unless tha kan hav the privilege ov splitting.

John Billings goes in bathing at Long Branch.—*See page 138.*

ON COURTING.

Courting is a luxury, it is sallad, it is ise water, it is a beveridge, it is the pla spell ov the soul. The man who has never courted haz lived in vain; he haz bin a blind man amung landskapes and waterskapes; he has bin a deff man in the land ov hand orgins, and by the side ov murmuring canals. Courting iz like 2 little springs ov soft water that steal out from under a rock at the fut ov a mountain and run down the hill side by side singing and dansing and spatering each uther, eddying and frothing and kaskading, now hiding under bank, now full ov sun and now full ov shadder, till bimeby tha jine and then tha go slow. I am in faver ov long courting; it gives the parties a chance to find out each uther's trump kards, it iz good exercise, and is jist as innersent as 2 merino lambs. Courting iz like strawberries and cream, wants tew be did slow, then yu git the flaver.

I hav saw folks git ackquainted, fall in luv, git marrid, settel down and git tew wurk, in 3 weeks from date. This is jist the wa sum folks larn a trade, and akounts for the grate number ov almitey mean mechanicks, we hav and the poor jobs tha turn out.

Perhaps it iz best i shud state sum good advise tew yung men, who are about tew court with a final view to matrimony, az it waz. In the fust plase, yung man, yu want tew git yure systen awl rite, and then find a yung woman who iz willing tew be courted on the square. The nex thing is tew find out how old she is, which yu kan dew bi asking her and she will sa that she is 19 years old, and this yu will find won't be far from out ov the wa. The nex best thing iz tew begin moderate; say onse evry nite in the week for the fust six months, increasing the dose as the pasheint seems to require it. It is a fust rate wa tew court the girl's mother a leetle on the start, for there iz one thing a woman never despizes, and that iz, a leettle good courting, if it is dun strikly on the square. After the fust year yu will begin to be well ackquainted and will begin tew like the bizzness. Thare is one thing I alwus advise, and that iz not to swop fotograffs oftener than onse in 10 daze, unless yu forgit how the gal looks.

Okasionally yu want tew look sorry and draw in yure wind az tho yu had pain, this will set the gal tew teazing yu tew find out what ails yu. Evening meetings are a good thing tu tend, it will keep yure religgion in tune; and then if the gal happens tew be thare, bi acksident, she kan ask yu tew go hum with her.

Az a ginral thing i wouldn't brag on uther gals mutch when i waz courting, it mite look az tho yu knu tew mutch. If yu will court 3 years in this wa, awl the time on the square, if yu don't sa it iz a leettle the slikest time in yure life, yu kan git measured for a hat at my expense, and pa for it. Don't court for munny, nor buty, nor relashuns, theze things are jist about az onsartin as the kerosene ile refining bissness, liabel tew git out ov repair and bust at enny minnit.

Court a gal for fun, for the luv yu bear her, for the vartue and bissness thare is in her; court her for a wife and for a mother, court her as yu wud court a farm — for the strength ov the sile and the parfeckshun ov the title; court her as tho she want a fule, and yu a nuther; court her in the kitchen, in the parlor, over the wash-tub, and at the pianner; court this wa, yung man, and if yu don't git a good wife and she don't git a good hustband, the falt won't be in the courting.

Yung man, yu kan rely upon Josh Billings, and if yu kant make these rules wurk jist send for him and he will sho yu how the thing is did, and it shant kost yu a cent.

LI.

REMARKS.

Piety iz a good kind ov dissease for a man tew hav, but when he has so mutch ov it that he has tew go behind the door on Sunday to drink his whiskee, it will dew tew watch him the rest of the week.

Menny think tha luv their husbands almost tew deth, when in fack, tha are only jealous ov them.

Thoze familys who are really fust class, never are afraid that tha shall git cheated out ov their respektability, while the codfish familys are alwus nervous lest tha mite.

The onla sure resipee tew govern mankind with, iz the rod; yu ma festoon it with flowers and case it with velvet, if yu pleze, but it iz the rod, after all, that duz the bizzness.

I kant conseive a more despikable opjek than a proud and arrogant man; he makes me think ov an old Tom Turkey trieing tew git mad at a red flannel pettycoat on a clothes line.

It iz not onla highly natral tew luv the femail sck, but 'tis highly pleasant.

Verry few people enjoy munny, bekauze tha kant git enuff ov it.

We are told that a contented man is happy, and we mite hav bin told, at the same, that a mudturkle could fly if it onla had wings.

It wont dew tew stir up a man when he is thinking, enny more than it will a pan ov milk when the cream is rising.

Thare is one time when awl men are comparitiffly pure, and that is when tha are in luv.

Humbolt was a man ov verry high attainments.

It iz eazy enuff tew raize the devil, but he iz a hard crop tew reap.

It appears tew me that a poor story iz a good deal like a grist, the oftner it iz told, the less thare iz ov it; but then, perhaps, i am mistaken.

I hav bin told that *swine Lager* iz the Dutch for root beer.

LII.

THE FAULT-FINDER.

Good Lord, deliver us from the Falt finder! one ov yure kronick grunters, i mean. Theze kind ov humin critters are alwuss full ov self consait; if tha waz humble and wud dam themself okasionally, i wud try tew pity them. Yure falt-finding old-bachelor, for instanze, odars a pair ov No. 8 boots, and then kolides with his shumaker insted ov his big feet; he walks tew the depo tew saive hack-hire and misses the trane, and then kolides with the time-table; he kourts a gal till she has tew marry sumboddy else tew keep from spileing, and then he don't believe thare is a vartuous woman living. If he enjoys ennything he dus it under protess, and if ennyboddy else enjoys ennything he knows tha lie about it. He is like a seckund rate bull tarrier, alwus a fiteing, and alwus gitting licked. These kind ov critters never are reddy tew die, bekause tha haint never begun tew live. I never maik their ackquaintanse enny more than i dew sumboddy's small pox, bekause i am a looking after bright things and haint got enny to lose. Thare aint enny remedee for this dissease but hunger, and that aint parmanent unless it results in starvashun. Good Lord, deliver us from the faltfinder! if yu undertake tew argy with them yu onla flatter them, and if yu jine in with them yu onla maik them mad with themselfs.

I had rather be a target for awl the bad luk in this wurld than tew go thru life shuteing a pizen arrow at awl the good luk. The more i think ov it, the more i keep thinking that falt-finding iz verry much like bobing for eels with a raw potater; a fust rate wa tew git out ov consait ov awl kinds ov fishing, and a fust rate wa not tew ketch enny eels.

LIII.

PROVERBS.

Chastity iz like an isikel. if it onse melts that's the last ov it.

Dew a good turn whenever yu kan even if yu hav tew turn sumboddy's grinstun tu dew it.

When a man dies the fust thing we talk about iz hiz welth, the nex thing hiz failings, and the last thing hiz vartues.

I suppose the "bone of contenshun" iz the collar bone.

An ungrateful childe is the revenge of Heaven.

After awl ced and dun the gran sekret of winning is tew win.

The studdy ov humin natur is a good deal like

the studdy ov dessekshun, yu finde out a good menny curis things, but it is a nasty job after awl.

When a man's dog deserts him on akount ov his poverty, he kant git enny lower down in this world, not bi land.

Sekrets maik a dungin of the harte, and a jailor ov its owner.

Don't let us forgit that the higher up we git the smaller will things look tew us here belo.

Natur haz no artifise, she plants her flowers in the gardin and in the wilderness, and endows them alike.

It iz tru that welth won't maik a man vartuous, but i notis thare ain't ennyboddy who wants tew be poor jist for the purpiss ov being good.

Luv iz like the meazels, we kant alwus tell when we ketched it and ain't ap tew hav it severe but onst, and then it ain't kounted mutch unless it strikes inly.

Tew be a suckcessful pollytysian, a man shud be butterd on both sides and then keep awa from the fire.

LIV.

KOLIDING.

The wurd "kolide," used bi ralerode men, haz an indefinit meaning tew menny folks. Thru the kindness of a nere and dear frend, i am able tew translate the wurd so that enny man ken understand it at onst. The term "kolide" is used tew explain the sarkumstanse ov 2 trains ov cars triing tew pass each uther on a single trak. It is ced that it never yet haz bin did suckcessfully, hence a "kolide."

JOSH BILLINGS.

LV.

ON SNAIKS AND MUDTURKLES.

I divide snaiks into one class, to wit, the devilish: They are ov much antiquity, having appeared about the same time that Adam did. The exact purpis for which tha was built hain't been explored yet; but one thing is sartin, tha are quite slippery and eazy to bend. Tha travel on thair bellys, and go down hill the moste eazyest; this is owing tew the fack that tha hain't got enny good rigging tew hold back with.

Snaix have but few warm friends, altho thare is folks who flatter them; sich persons ought tew be obliged to ware a pair ov them for a cravat. Thare is but one thing that makes me more horrible than a striped snaik, and that is a big black one jest sliding away from the place whare I was going tew sit down on the grass.

We are told that Eve waz sedused bi a snaik, i don' beleave thare is a woman living now, in theze parts, that it could be did tew without spileing the snaik. I hav bin in the habit, ov late years, ov sedusing snaiks miself evvry chanse i could git; i ginerally dew it bi gitting them tew put their heds under a stone, and then i cruelly desert them; sich is life!

Snaiks are amphibicus and thoze which dwell in the water are called eels. Tha are ov awl cullers, and sum are pizen tew behold; amung theze are the koperheds, but tha never bite enny ov their own folks. Snaiks hav got a big appertite, akordin tew their size; i hav saw them no thicker than your finger, with 4 inches wide ov toad in them, tha stuck out like 2 quarts ov milk that had got into a young pup bi acksident.

The largest snaik in the wurld iz kept at Newport, he iz owned bi the landlords, he never haz bin shown tew but one person tew a time, and then he is generally 110 feet long; thousands go thare tew see him summers, and pay 3 dollars a da for board and 2 dollars a week tew the servants for something tew eat.

I beleave a snaik never dies onla bi mistake, and never ventures out mutch in the winter when the travling iz bad, and lays eggs like a small hen, but don't set on them bekauze tha hain't got enny more heat in their body than a ramrod haz.

ON SNAIKS AND MUDTURKLES.

Almoste evry humin being haz got a nateral appertite agin snaix, and i will bet, if you shud put a striped snaik in a 10 aker lot, whare there was 27 wimmin picking strawberries, and holler out, "striped snaik! striped snaik!" evry woman would skream, and go to feeling rite oph for the snaik. It is ced that snaik ile applied to the back·ov a man's neck, will cure him from lieing. This is wuth trieing, even if it wont wurk, but mi individoal presentiment iz, that when the lieing disease gits familiar with a man, deth alone will put an eend to his sufferings. But I dont want it understood that I am agin snaik ile, for this one reason if no other, the more snaik ile there is in the market, the less snaiks.

MUDTURKLES.

Mudturkles liv in a shell, which tha git verry mutch attached to. Tha are not fond ov company, and seldom receive visitors in their houses. Their food consists prinsipally of what they eat, which tha find wharever tha kan git it. Their style iz haf land, and haf water, and tha are at home on the banks or at the bottom ov a kanal. Tha hav sum eggs, which tha lay in sum warm sand, and ginerally hav them hatched out tew the halves. Tha belong tew the class known az "close korporashuns," and are a hard animil tew whip, bekause tha alwus fite under cover. The mudturkle kant climb very well, and therefore seldum iz found up a tree. Tha are verry tuff ov life, and will outlive an injun rubber shoe, and don't seem tew gro old enny faster than a paving stone duz. Tha kan be domestikated without enny trubble; awl yu hav tew dew, iz tew put them into a barrel, and tha aint ap tew stray off far. Mudturkles hav their faults, but tha won't lie, nor drink rum, nor chaw terbacker, and tho tha cant trot as fast az sum hosses kan, thare sure tew git tew whare tha go tew, and never brake down on the rode. I take a deep interest in moste awl the animils, and particularly in mudturkles, and i dew hope that the Legislature in their wisdum won't pass a law "prohibiting enny more mudturkles." I regret tew hear, that in sum parts ov the kuntry, the people are in the habit of using mudturkles tew pitch quoits with, but I think this wants an affidavy with a revenew stamp onto it.

In theze mi remarks about snaix and mudturkles i hav tried hard tew tell the truth, but if i hav failed, it is owing tew the grate skasity ov truth in theze days.

LVI.

TRUE BILLS.

Tru dignity is the effeck ov the conscious possession ov ability and vartue. False dignity is the effeck ov nu clothes, no branes and mutch vittles.

Tru currage is the knowledge ov right and the determination tew dew it. False currage is a willingness tew dew what is rong bekauze others sa it iz right.

Tru religgun iz tew fear God, love man and hate the devil. False religgun iz tew hate God, fear man and luv the devil.

True faith is a parfeck trust in what we are satisfied iz truth. False faith is a craziness tew beleave, simpla bekauze we kant understand.

Tru liberta is the possession ov our own rights and due respek for the rights ov uthers. False liberta iz a desire tew possess uther's rights and no respek for our own.

Tru wisdum iz a plenta ov experiense, observashun and reflekshun. False wisdom iz a plenta ov ignorance, arogance and impudence.

LVII.

NARRATIF.

Wunce as I was travling thru tioga keounty, a peddlin, selebrated pills," I was akosted by a individual whose dress indikated, that he was in the kolporter bisness. We met, and stopped smoltaneously, as it war; we looked into each others phases, sarching as it war, for a linamont, a oasus, that we nu, or had hearn tell of, but the trak pedlar, and pill pedlar, had evidently met for the first time on arth. The dela that was thus instituted, giv me a margin for a clus communion with the kolporturs feturs, and stile of habiliment, and tru to natur, tuk the chance — he was about 59 years old, was very lite in the karkass, and wore his close very much as a methodis dus, and had one of them kountenances that Moses was celebrated for. I felt at the first site, that he wud do tu ti to. He komensed as follers: — "Wafarin man, monament of sparin mersa, du yu feel as tho yu had enny intrest in yurself, hev yu ever been tried by the fire that takes awa the spiritoal dross, and had yur soal a flutterin agin the ribbid prisin bars of yur body, like a kaged song bird of heavin? If yu haint, read and peroose this trak; the ile that it kontains, will permoate thru the resesses of yur hart, like the quicksilver of luv, and lukrubrate the loose roaling stuns, that ly in yur jordanick pathwa." As he cum to a stop, he bent on tu me one of those meller looks, that a tom kat gives tu the mouse, as it lays pantin afore him, with a skin full of broken bones, and a reachin around, he pulled from his sadle bags, a trak of four pages, and give it tu me, with (if I ma be aloud the expresshun) a angelik tenderness, and as he did so, he karlessly tuk a look at my hoss, who stood quietly in the harness, a restin wun of his hine fete. I thanked him, and sed I wud peroose the trak, an hoped to find the ile, and silver, he spoak of. Not tu be bete in generosity, I opened the lid of mi waggin, and selekted a box of pills, with a full kount, and arisin from mi sete, I kommenced as follers, " respected kolportur, allou me tu disiprookate, by plasin at yur disposal a full kount box, of the selebrated antydiluvion pills, begot by Josh Billings (late of this tioga keounty,) who now stans befoor yu. These pills are friendla tu the innards of enny man, are holy made of rootes, are as saif tu take as a fotograph, and at the same time, are as thoro as a sarch warrant, there ar 26 ov them in a box, an tha sel, with a ful size fax similer of the author on the lid ov the box. He tuk the antydiluvions, and summed up as follers, " docter Billings, the perfeshun which you hav chose, is wone ov the most anshient as wel as wone of the most humain, it speaks volumes in yur praze, and as i winde mi wa on errants of soal mersa, upon mi noble hoss (whose only falt, or rather misfortin is a paneful saddil gaul,) swete gushes of jowus thout will wel up from mi happer harte, that praps our auspicious meeting tu da ma bee the menes of awakin in yu, a arnest kry what shal i du tu bee saved." At the kloze ov this speach, i wud have bin willin tu bet a Box of antydiluvions agin a 10 rowed papir of solid headed pins, that the kolporter was nasty on a hoss swap, and i kum tu the konklusion that i wud just feal of his stile in that wa. Pretendin tu hav just notised his hoss i went inter fits over the diskivery, and soon found i had struc a lead, for the star spangle bannor, never had at one time enny more sed in its praze, than the kolporter let of in favor ov his old hoss. Not edzackly disposed tu swaller, without stirrin, all he sed, i thout i wud look the kritter over, and jumpin out ov my waggin, fur that purpis, soon found out that the trak pedler was after Jonas, insted of me. After i had got the full size of the sarkumstanses in the kase, i kum tu one of the brisk konklusions that the Billings family are subject tu, by hintin in oktave, " that the kolporter was a dam hiperkrit, and his spavined hoss a dam old pelter." This suddint bust of centiment on mi part, awoke the sleapin pieta of the trak pedlar, and he at wunst tuk me tu do for swarin. After i had told him, that his prain and my swarin, was oph of the same peace, an neather ov us ment any thing we sed, we parted,— the kolporter to save soals, and swap hosses, and Josh Billings tu sell, for 25 sents a box, the antidiluvion pills, as saif as rute beer, and as sartin as the bight ov a mogasin.

LVIII.

PHOTOGRAPHS.

Enclosed yu will be pleazed tew find my fotograff, taken from life, on the spot, whare the circumstanze occurred. I take the liberta tew send yu the picter, for the 7 different ensuing reasons: 1 — Photograffs are gitting skase. 2 — If you should ever meet me by mistake, yu wud be able to kno me rite oph, bi asking me if I resembled the pictur. 3 — I am a marrid man, and am the author ov a familee, and therefore the danger ov any femail fallin in luv with me, bi cuming in contak with the picter, will be painfully redused. 4 — It iz better that 99 humbly cusses should eskape, than that one decent looking man should suffer bi not having hiz fotograff taken. 5 — A grate menny folks, jist now at this time, are troubled with a literature on the brane. This pictur will put yu in clus communion with a man who haz had this diseaze, but who haz so far rekovered, that he iz able to sit up and laff at others, who are trieing to ketch the same disorder. 6 — I resembel this pictur, and that ken be ced ov so few things in this wurld, that i thought noboddy would git mad and call me a verry d — n fule, for sirkulating the pictur. 7 — The artiss said I was hard tew take, and this pictur was a triumph ov the art; he alzo added that some ware so eazy tew take that it was actooally dangerous tew leave ennything in their reach. These reasons must be mi excuse for sending yu my pictur; if it don't look as yu expekted i did, jist let me kno, and i will have one taken that duz. Verry highly i remane yures,

JOSH BILLINGS.

Josh Billings having stopped to kiss the baby once more, arrives at the depôt just too late to catch the Express train (?).—*See page 166.*

LIX.

AFFERISIMS.

I suppoze the reazon why wimmin are so fast talkers, is bekause tha dont hav tew stop tew spit on their hands.

After Joseph's bretheren had beat him out ov hiz cut ov menny cullers, what did tha dew nex? Tha pittied him!

Thare is nothing in this life that will open the pores ov a man so mutch, as tew fall in luv, it makes him fluent as a tin whissell, as limber as a boy's watch chain, and as perlite as a dansing master; his harte is as full ov sunshine as a hay field, and there aint any more guile in him than there is in a stik ov merlasses candy.

Thare dont seem tew be enny end tew the ambishun ov men, but thare is one thing that sum ov them will find out if tha ever dew get tew heaven, and that is tha cant git enny further.

He who kan hold awl tu gits, kan most generally git more.

Conshense, is onla another name for truth.

Yu kant alwus tell a gentleman by his clothes, but yu kan bi his finger nails.

Adam invented "*Luv at first sight*," one ov the gratest laber saving masheens the world ever saw.

It is a grave question whether, in curtailing superfluitys in these hard times, we have a moral right tew cut oph a dorg's tale tew save the expense ov boarding it.

Are Greenbacks a lawful tender? If yu dont believe it tri one on me, espeshila one ov the heavy ones.

Dont never parade yure good luck, nor yure bad

luck before men, the first will make them think less ov *yu*, and the second will make them think more of *themselves*.

Thare are a grate multitude ov individuals who are like blind mules, anxious enough to kick, but kant tell whare.

I hav herd a grate deal ced about *"broken hartes,"* and thare may be a fu ov them, but mi experiense is that nex tew the gizzard, the harte is the tuffest peace ov meat in the whole critter.

LX.

JOSH GITS ORFULLY BIT

I du consider musketers,
The moste pesky, ov all God's creeters.

I hav finally ketched it. I hav bin like a lam led suddeu tu the slauter and had mi blood sucked out ov me, az though it waz only sweet sider, and belonged tu sumbody else. I am a man ov peace, but low, and behold! there aint a peace in me now, but what iz bit, punkterd, and tore.

When muskeeters whisper in yure ear,
The devils angels are hovring near.

I retired laste nite tu rest, at the usual time; on the north side ov me, and about 2 feet adjacent, waz the side ov the hous, on the south side ov me, and about 2 feet adjacent la mi wife. I dropt tu sleep, az a snoflake dus on the buzzum ov a silvery Lake, (i have a faint idee that this laste sentense, for lovlaness, kant be beat, handy.) I dreamed a good-sized, hot dream.

> It felt like the breth ov a kanada Thissell,
> A round mi hed, a triing tu Whissell

Suddenly i awoke.

The room waz full ov yels, and skreams. responsiv I dashed wildly akross the room, ackompanied by mi shirt tale. i lit a lite. I harked, one ov mi moste reliable harks. Awl waz still; still az a crows nest, in the ded ov winter. I gazed a gaze, az tho i waz triing tu thread the rong end ov a kambrik needle. Awa in the distance, solitara, and alone, clus up tu the ceiling, chawing hiz cud, sot a little grey cuss. I dipped a koars towel into a basen ov water, and rung it out, i krept up under the little grey cuss, i tuk aim, and fired,

> And hit the spot,
> Whare the little grey cuss had sot.

Awl waz still again. I onlighted the kandle, and saught mi kouch.

LXI.

THINGS THAT SUIT ME.

I like an aimabel man, (not one who will let yu spit on him,) but one who don't want tew spit on enny boddy else

I like a stirring man, (not one who stirs up musses,) but one who haz got sumthing tew dew and duz it.

I like a good looking man, (not a pretty man), but one who looks well — into things, one whom yu can't phule with a mare's nest, unless he sees the old mare on it.

I like a gritty man, (not a dirty one), but one that pitches in like a frog oph from a saw log, no matter how deep the water iz.

THINGS THAT SUIT ME.

I like a fass hoss, (one that goes fass bekauze he luvs tew), sich a critter iz half human; he never ought to be hitched tew a plough, he ought tew be took out ov hiz stable az a wild pigeon had out of hiz cage, and let him — go.

I like a rat tarrier with hiz hair awl combed forward, hiz eyes on fire, hiz tale straight out stiff, evry muscle alive, and the entire dorg only 3 feet off from a rat hole.

I like a woman, (handsum if it iz convenient,) with more wisdum than larning, chaste, but not frozen, soft, but not silly, and fond, but not fussy, sich wimmin are skase, and are going tew be skaser.

I like religion, (the kind that wurks 6 days and rests on the 7,) which acks on a man's soul, az congriss water duz on hiz boddy, phesicks him well, but dont make him enny weaker.

I like good order — good morals — good frends — and awl things well dun, except beefsteak, and that I want rare dun.

LXII.

MY FUST GONG.

I never kan eradicate holy from mi memry the sound ov the first gong I ever herd — i was setting on the frunt stupe ov a tavern in the sitty ov Bufferlo, pensively a smokin. The sun was a goin tu bed, and the heavens fur and nere was blushing at the purformanse. The Eri kanall with its goldin waters was on its windin wa tu albany, and i was perusin the line botes, a flotin by, and thinkin ov Italy, (whare i used tu live,) and her gondolers, and gallus wimmin. Mi entire sole was, as it ware in a swet, i wanted tu climb, i felt grate, i aktually grew. Thar ar things in this life tu big tu be trifled with, thar ar times when a man brakes luce from hisself, when he sees speerits, when he kan almost tuch the moon, and feels as tho he kud fill both hands with the stars ov heavin and almost sware he was a bank president. Thats what ailed me. But the korse ov tru luv never did run

MY FIRST GONG.

smoove, (this iz Shakesperes opinion too, i and he often think thru one quill) just az i was duing my best, · · · · dummer, dummer, spat, bang, beller, crash, roar, ram, dummer, dummer, whang, rip, rare rally; dummer dummer, dummer dum, · · · · with one tremenjis jump, i struck the senter ov the side walk, with anuther i kleared the gutter and with anuther, i stud in the middle ov the strets snorting like a injin poney, at a band ov musik; i gazed in wilde dispare at the tavern stand, mi harte swelled up as big as an out door oven, mi teeth were as luce as a string ov prairy beads. I thout all the crokery in the tavern stand had fell down, i thout ov fenomenoms, i thought ov gabrel and his horn. i was just on the pint ov thinking ov sumthing else when the landlord cum out to the frunt stupe ov the tavern stand holding by a string the bottom ov an old brass kittle. He called me gentla with his hand i went slola and sadla tu him, he calmed mi feres, he ced it was a gong; i saw the cussed thing, he ced supper was reddy, he axed me if i would hav black or green tea and i ced i would.

LXIII.

PROVERBS.

Up-and-down men are skase, but the horizontal are less skaser.

Thare iz sum disseazes that kant be kured even bi deth, for we oftin see them brake out on a man's tombstun more violent than ever.

The *burden* ov menny ov the songs that are ritten iz the song itself.

Thare iz no better kompliment tew vartue than this : "That Vise alwus konkocts her grate plans in the naim ov vartue."

The tempel ov Fame iz lokated on an exceeding hi mountin, and yu hav got tew fli or kreep tew git tew it. (N. B. This provarb haz bin ced before, and ain't one ov mine, but it iz jiss as tru as tho it was.)

Buty iz a short suckcess, but while it lastes it iz quite pretty.

"The *flour* ov the familee," iz, alas! quite oftin a little injun.

If innersense iz onla the result ov ignoranse, it ain't enny more one ov the vartues than buty iz; but if it iz the effek ov eddikashun it iz the queen ov the vartues.

Vartue needs awl the enemys she haz got, tew keep her tools bright and in order.

I never beleaved mutch in *spirits* unless tha kum direk from Jamaka, and then onla in small-sized ones.

"Absense ov mind;" about 2 thirds ov the humin rase are trubbled with this kalamitee.

It taiks 2 tew maik a bargin; it ought tew taik 2 tew brake it.

Yu ma differ as mutch as yu plese about the stile ov a yung lady's figger, but i tell yu konfidenshally, if she has got $40,000, the figger is about as near rite as yu wil git it.

"Glory enuff for one day;" attending a kamp meeting.

Goldsmith sez, "Larn the luxury ov dewing good;" but the luxury, now a daze, consiss in larning how tew du a leetle better.

I often hear affekshunate husbands kall their wifes "Mi Duck," i wunder if this ain't a sli delusion tew their big bills?

LXIV.

DISIPLIN IZ EVRATHING — IN 2 PARTS.

Part Fust — I dont suppoze thare is enny dout about this assershun. A man who haint got propper disiplin, iz jist about ov az mutch uze tew hiz fellow critters az a wether cock wud be amung a parcil ov barnyard pulletts. Injuns haint got enny disciplin, and, konsequentla, the more injuns a man had tew run a kotton faktory with, the wus he wud be oph. Turning a grinstone iz fust rate disiplin. If a man ov ornary mind haint got disiplin, he bekums a lofer the fust good chanse he gits. Thare haz bin, perhaps, a fu individoals born into the world that did'nt want mutch disiplin — Homer, and Virgil, and Shakesper, and sich like, if tha had bin sot to turning a grinstone it mite hav spilt them — tha waz like Eagles, made tu fli without enny praktis. Disiplin iz evrathing. The thurer bred Hoss wants the smoothe bit ov disiplin — the mule wants the sled-stake disiplin.

Part Seckunt.—Majer Spenser had leaf ov abscense from his regiment, and was glad enuff, i tell yu, tew swap the pesky air ov the suthern konfederasy for the brittle breth ov Nu England. He spent his time a climeing the mountains ov his natiff land, and looking way down into the hollers; he worryed the trouts as tha swum up and down hill in the brooks, and he gethered penroyal for his good old Ma tu hang up in the wood hous chamber, tew make arb tea ov next winter. Majer Spenser had a brother who was a minister ov the gospil, and the Majer boarded with him. One Sunda nite the minister and the Majer sot kommuning together. The moon cum up out ov the East, as big as an old fashund kart wheel (one ov the ox kind ov kart wheels, i mean,) the stars stuk clean out ov the ski, and the air was filled with the musick ov the cows a chawing their cuds in the distance. All natur la undisturbed. "Brother," ced Parson, a braking the paws, "how did yu like divine sarvice to-day?" Very well, sir, very well, sir," ced the Majer, "*if that dam deakin ov yurs hadn't refused to pra when yu asked him. Disiplin, sir, disiplin iz evry thing.*

LXV.

CORRESPONDENTS.

Olivia — I never have visited the Mormons, but my friend Artemus Ward has, and he tells me they are a healthy people, and fond ov femail society. He says they hav more religion, akordin to their populashun, than tha kno what to dew with. They marry young and often. The produkshun ov the country iz Mormons. They beleaf in a hereafter, but it iz genrally a hereafter of wimmin. They are fond ov amusements, sich az pitching cents and sliding down hill.

Scipio — If I had the dyspepsy I would buy me a hard trotting hoss, (off from the kanawl,) and ride him bare back 40 miles a day for a spase ov time. If that didn't seem tew influense me, I would soke in cold water for 12 months. If that didn't seem tew influense me, I would issue proposals tew the lowest bidder to be fed for one year on bran bred and slippery elm tea. If that didn't seem tew influense me, I would sell my house and lot, and invest the proceeds in pattent medisin, and take the whole lot in rotashun. If that didn't seem tew influense me, I would cum tew the konklusion that I had the water brash, or some other thing, I didn't care which, and take a job ov thrashing out wet rye for evry tenth bushel, and git — well.

Clarence — We never undertake tew return rejekted manuskrip. The fact iz, we don't read more than half we reject. It iz a way we hav got.

Matty —- It iz very natral that you should ask me in what manner you should reseave the proposal from your lover. It iz sumthing ov a trick tew dew it nice. You don't ought tew jump into the collar suddin, nor fly back suddin, like a bocky hoss, but yu ought tew take it kind, looking down hill, with an expreshun, about half tickled and half scart. After the pop iz over, if your luvver wants tew kiss you, I dont think I would say yes or no, but let the thing kind ov take its own course. There iz one thing I hav alwus stuck tew, and that iz, give me long courtships and engagements.

Stujent—We never furnish ortograffs in less quantity than bi the package. It iz a bizness that grate men hav got into, but it dont strik us az being profitable nor amuzing. We furnished a near and very dear friend our ortograff a few years ago, for 90 days, and it got into the hands ov one of the banks, and it kost us $275 tew get it back. We went out of the bizzness then, and have not hankered for it sinse.

LXVI.

JOSH BILLINGS AT SARATOGA SPRINGS.

It will probely fill you with an arnest solisitude for mi fate, az it dus me with emoshuns of stupenjus grander, tu find miself at this grate modern Siloam, this august whirlpool ov wine, wimmin and hosses; this fairy sceen ov poetry, dreams, and natural fisick. Upon mi arival, i took immegiate rooms at the tavern called the "*Union* now and forever," and commensed at onst tu kreate a sensashun — " Dignatum hok hanimum disisimo." This centiment is from the Chocktaw ov Raphael, and is one ov mi faverite quotashuns.

The town is about haf full ov folks, menny of them hav been highly renowned. I kould name them personaly by name, but this wud look like affekshun in me, az tha hav alreddy sent in their kard, and begged the privilege ov kalling on me, at mi moste soonest spare time. It will be impossible for me, my amiable friends, tu give yu ennything like a well digested orashun, ov the eckstatick wonders that hover around me, among which i am permitted tu menshun the pensiv modesta ov the unmarried; the gushing rapture ov the married; the shadowy tenderness ov the widders, and the universal fisick that fills up the pauzes. Theze are subjecks which hav bin writ onto so much that all the good things haz bin said.

It iz a source ov grate pride tu see so menny here from youre citty, and what fills me with gratitude tu an overruling Providence, iz the fac that their festiv naturs develop into such lovelyness here; thare iz dekon L——, and Elder P——, for instanze, with whom i take a drink evry time tha ask me. I think now that i shall remain here for sevral years. I am allmost sorry i didn't bring mi jewelry trunk with me; i'll bet i could hav sold a thousand Dollars worth a da, ov brest pins. It iz a fust rate place here tu buy hosses cheap. i waz offered 2 carriage hosses for onla 25 hundred dollars; i shud hav tuk them, but i couldn't hire enny boddy tu take them hum for me. There iz a grate menny here who talk with a forrin tung. I am trieing it. My wife laffs at me, and kalls me "her dark komplekted one!"— Tha hav got here alreddy tu or three billyard tabils in suckcessful operrashun, and i am told that, if pease iz declared, nex season tha intend tu start a 10-pin allee.

Congriss Spring is lokated here; it tasts verry much like sumthing or ruther, i kant tell which, and iz now generally admitted tu be kartharticus. I am partiklar impressed with the moral centiment that pervades things here. I am told a man wanted tu hire a room tu gamble in with dominoze, but the authoritize immejiately burnt him in effigee. Dimonds are trumps here, and menny good hands are held. Thare is no end tu the number ov selebrated belles here. Thare is one that cums out about 3 o'clock every day, that takes them all down. I allude now in a kind ov burleskish wa tu the *dinner*-bell. But, after all, Solomon gits mi time when he bust out in this fashun, "All is vanitee and vexashun of spirits." Good for Solomon! Mi christain friends, good-bi. JOSH BILLINGS.

LXVII.

NOT ENNY SHANGHI FOR ME.

The shanghi ruseter is a gentile, and speaks in a forrin tung. He is bilt on piles like a Sandy Hill crane. If he had bin bilt with 4 legs, he wud resembel the peruvian lama. He is not a game animil, but quite often cums off sekund best in a ruff and tumble fite; like the injuns, tha kant stand sivilization, and are fast disappearing. Tha roost on the ground, similar tew the mud turkle. Tha oftin go to sleep standing, and sum times pitch over, and when tha dew, tha enter the ground like a pickaxe. Thare food consis ov korn in the ear. Tha crow like a jackass, troubled with the bronskeesucks. Tha will eat as mutch tu onst as a district skule master, and ginerally sit down rite oph tew keep from tipping over. Tha are dredful unhandy tew cook, yu hav tu bile one eend ov them tu a time, yu kant git them awl into a potash kittle tu onst. The femail ruster lays an eg as big as a kokernut, and is sick for a week afterwards, and when she hatches out a litter of yung shanghis she has tew brood them standing, and then kant kiver but 3 ov them — the rest stand around on the outside, like boys around a cirkus tent, gitting a peep under the kanvas when ever tha kan. The man who fust brought the breed into this kuntry ought tew own them all and be obliged tew feed them on grasshoppers, caught bi hand. I never owned but one and he got choked tu deth bi a kink in a clothes line, but not until he had swallered 18 feet ov it. Not enny shanghi for me, if yu pleze; i wuld rather board a travelling kolporter, and as for eating one, giv me a biled owl rare dun, or a turkee buzzard, roasted hole, and stuffed with a pair ov injun rubber boots, but not enny shanghi for me, not a shanghi!

LXVIII.

IS DISPOSING OV THINGS FOR CHARITABEL PURPOSES BI "LOT" A SIN?

EXAMINED BY JOSH BILLINGS.

Fustly — I think it is a sin. So it is a sin tew dew a sin, that good may cum out ov it, but the good that comes out ov it aint a sin, is it? Ha!

Sekundly — I think it is a sin onse more. So i think the manefakter ov sider brandee is a sin, but the use ov it tew kure the rhumatiz aint a sin mutch.

Thirdly — I think it is a sin onse morely. So is this war a sin, but we awl of us are in hopes that its fruits will be righteousness, and righteousness aint no sin.

Fourthly — I keep thinking that it is a sin. So is cutting oph a dog's tale tew keep it from gitting stepped on, a sin, but it dont hurt the dog for ketching rats, duz it?

Fifthly and *lastly*, i kno it is a sin. Bekase awl those who make the most fuss about it, are the verry ones, who if tha shud be misled into buying a tiket for one dollar and didn't draw a mowing masheen, wud feal rite off as tho the Lord warnt on their side.

Moral.— Dont engage in a "Lot," unless yu are parfekly willing the Lord shud have the tiket and the mowing masheen too.

"Not enny Shanghi for me, not enny."—*See page* 189

LXIX.

ADVERTIZEMENT.

I kan sell for eighteen hundred and thirty-nine dollars, a pallas, a sweet and pensive retirement, lokated on the virgin banks ov the Hudson, kontaining 85 acres. The land is luxuriously divided by the hand of natur and art, into pastor and tillage, into plain and deklivity, into stern abruptness, and the dallianse ov moss-tufted medder; streams ov sparkling gladness, (thick with trout,) danse through this wilderness ov buty, tew the low musik ov the kricket and grasshopper. The evergreen sighs az the evening zephir flits through its shadowy buzzum, and the aspen trembles like the luv-smitten harte ov a damsell. Fruits ov the tropicks, in golden buty, melt on the bows, and the bees go heavy and sweet from the fields to their garnering hives. The manshun iz ov Parian marble, the porch iz a single diamond, set with rubiz and the mother ov pearl; the floors are ov rosewood, and the ceilings are more butiful than the starry vault of heavin. Hot and cold water bubbles and squirts in evry apartment, and nothing is wanting that a poet could pra for, or art could portray. The stables are worthy of the steeds ov Nimrod or the studs ov Akilles, and its henery waz bilt expressly for the birds of paradice; while somber in the distance, like the cave ov a hermit, glimpses are caught ov the dorg-house. Here poets hav cum and warbled their laze — here skulptors hav cut, here painters hav robbed the scene ov dreamy landskapes, and here the philosopher diskovered the stun, which made him the alkimist ov natur. Nex northward ov this thing ov buty, sleeps the residense and domain ov the Duke John Smith; while southward, and nearer the spice-breathing tropicks, may be seen the barronial villy ov Earl Brown, and the Duchess, Widder Betsy Stevens. Walls ov primitiff rock, laid in Roman cement, bound the estate, while upward and downward, the eye catches far away, the magesta and slow grander ov the Hudson. As the young morn hangs like a cutting ov silver from the blu brest ov the ski, an angel may be seen each night dansing with golden tiptoes on the grecn. (N. B. This angel goes with the place.)

Biagrams kan be seen at the offiss ov the broker. Terms flattering. None but principals delt with. Title as pure as the breth ov a white male infant, and possession given with the lark. For more full deskripshun, read Ovid's Art ov Luv, or kall (in yure carriage) on Josh Billings, Real Estate Agent.

LXX.

OUT WEST!

Tha sa the praree chickens are so thik, out West, tha hav tew put up poles awl over the kuntry for them tew roost on.

When tha bust up, out there, tha pay their debts, by jineing the church.

It being agin the law tew carry consealed weepons, evry man carrys one in his hand.

A man who don't kno how tew pla uker, would not be believed under oath.

It iz 5 dollars fine, in Cinsinnatti, tew strike a hog, in anger.

Tha don't bore for ile, out thare, tha bore for whiskee, and hav the best luk in the visinity ov the graveyards.

In sum parts, out West, it iz almoste unpossibel tew git water; one man in Pike County dug a well 90 feet deep, and then struk a bed ov sawdust; he put in an injine, and iz pumping out a 1000 bushel a da, which he sells tew the Government, for hoss feed.

The prinsipal produkshuns or the kuntry are, whiskee in the ear, and rale rode stok in the bundle.

LXXI.

SAYINS.

About the only difference between the poor and the ritch, is this, the poor *suffer* mizery, while the ritch hav tu *enjoy* it.

"Bee yee as wize as a sarpint, and as harmlis as a duve," and then if a feller cums a fooling around yure duve, yu kan set yure sarpint at him.

Rize arly, work hard, and late, live on what yu kant sell, giv nothing awa, and if yu dont die ritch, and go tu the devil, yu ma sue me for damages.

Marrin for love ma be a little risky, but it is so honest, that God kant help but smile on it.

There is one thing I kant never forgit nor I hain tried to, and that is, the fust time I kissed a gal.

If I was asked, "what is the chief end of man now a daze," I should immegiatly repli, "10 per cent."

Yu may argy a bull Tarrier out ov a bone, but yu kant argy a woman out ov her will.

Mi advise tu them who are about tu begin, in arnest, the jurney ov life, is tu take their harte in one hand and a club in the other.

The biggest glutton I ever herd tell ov, was the feller out in Indianny, who eat a pair ov twin lams for brekfast, and then chased the ole yew three miles and a haf.

The peacock has one ov the most butifullest tails in the world, but i tak notis he dont drag it on the ground when he walks out.

LXXII.

A WIMMIN'S LEAGUE MEETIN.

I don't kno when i hav bin filled so near up tew the brim with a fond feelink for the fair sek az i was last nite at mi natiff plase, the good old borough ov Billingsville, whither i had gone on a visit tew git mi boots tapped. The wimmin had called a meetin' ov the fair sekts tew take into konsiderashun the propriety ov not wareing enny more clothes, that is, forrin bilt clothes. The meetin waz got into shape bi kalling Mrs. Peleg Pewter tew the chair. The fust thing she did waz tew create a silence, which she did after about 30 minnits, awl excep a fu whispering, which she could not dry up.

The style ov the meetin' having bin sot up in big type bi the Mrs. Pcleg Pewter, she ced thare waz an opening, and no less than 4 wimmin started for the opening at onst; but the president decided that Mrs. Cynthee Coon waz about one neck ahed, and

A WIMMIN'S LEAGUE MEETIN. 201

tharefore, waz entitled tew the fust heat. She waz a woman about 14 hands hi, and wore wollen stockings. She ced she waz for home manafakter and waz agin awl luxury excep a nu shawl, and that she must hav. She ced she waz willing tew giv up silk, but she must hav 1 more nu shawl if it bust her.

She ced she thought thare ought tew be sum diskriminashun between what folks didn't want and what tha did, and for her part she was reddy tew go her length or ennyboddy else's length agin the noshun that poor people had ov hankering after imported goods.

Her speech lasted for about 2 hours, and was listened to with breathless expense. When she sot down the wimmin gathered around her; sum ov them held camphor tew her noze, sum ov them unhooked her dress, and one ov them, more thoughtful than the rest, mixed up a gin sling, which she struggled with for a minnit, and then ced it did her soul good. A committee ov 3 ov the heavyest wimmin was appointed bi the chair with power tew draw up a sett ov resolushuns which was reported as follows:

Whereas, resolved, that silks, and shawls, and so orth, are a luxury from imported kuntrys, and we are down on them.

Resolved, that we are down on silks and shawls.

Resolved, that we wont uze silks and shawls onla in case ov sickness.

Resolved, that the foregoing resolushuns be published 3 times a week in the *Billingsville Weekly*, and that our husbands foot the bills or we foot them — the bills.

Resolved, that we pledg ourselfs, our fortins, and our natiff land, tew sustane the above sett ov resolushuns.

After taking a pinch ov snuff, and kissing awl around, the meeting broke up tew meet " sine die " on the next Teusday. · · · · · Ov course no male man was allowed at the meetin', but i receaved a koppa ov the resolushuns the nex morning, accompanyed with mi respeks.

LXXIII.

A TRUE FISH STORY FOUNDED ON FAK

In a little town awa out wes whar i used tew liv, thare wast two elders resided. One ov them wast a Babtiss, Gaffit bi name, and the other wast a Methodis, Sturgiss bi name, and both ov them wast as good fellers as ever sarved the Lord. As good luk wud hav it tha both had a revival ov religion in their floks at the same time. Gaffit was a cunning critter, besides being as harmless as the duv. Thare was but one pond in the town, and that was used for babtizing by agreement, on wensday ov each week, bi Gaffit, and on saturday bi Sturgiss. One wensday, as Gaffit was engaged in marking his sheep, or in uther wurds, was bi the side ov the little pond ov water adminstering the rite ov babtism tew a goodla number, whom he had coaxed awa from the wiles ov the devil, Sturgiss looked in upon the happy scene, with eys brimful ov luv. Amung the menny who ware waiting tew be babtized, Sturgiss diskovered sevral whom he had convikted, and whom he expetked tew add tew his flok on the cumming saturda. The nex da the two elders met, Sturgiss charged Gaffit with the pious fraud he had detekted bi the side ov the little pond. Gaffit's eyes puckered with delite, as he listened tew the charge, then seezin the methodis elder bi the hand with an extra pucker in his eye, whispered: "Brother Sturgiss, mi father larnt me when i was but a little fisher-boy, tew string mi fish as fast as i ketched 'em."

LXXIV.

AT SARATOGA SPRINGS.

I arrived here nite before last at arly kandle lite. Mi wife and 2 children ackompanyed me. The fust thing that i did was tu call for a tavern; i got one immegiately, and took a room, from choice, in the Seventh story, all the rooms above wer took. The tavern whare i stop, is called the Union, one, and inseprable. The bar is stocked with the choicest lickers. Thare must be 3 or 4 hundred black serviants here, tha all wear white aporns, and hav their hair curled clos. The tavern keeper rings a gong with a klub when the vittles is reddy, and then the boarders march in; 'tis a moste effecting site! I havent et enynthing yet but briled chickens. I gess evry body here knows me, tha look at me so. I kreated a sensashun yesterday after dinner, on the front stupe ov the tavern, by calling a cullard servant tu pick mi teeth. I herd one ov the ladys sa, "i was an English Lord, she had saw me at Nuport laste seson." I shall sta here as long as i can injuce mi females tu remain. This is the place where the congriss water cums from; tha dip it up out ov a hole in the ground, with a roof over it, you can drink 4 or 5 tumblers ov it tu onst, without swallering; it tastes a good deal like sumthing i never tasted before, and it operates on the inwards for all the world, just like pills. It dus look so funny tu see 8 or 9 hundred mails, and femails, all taking fisick tu once; 'tis a pensiv sight! The town kontains about 6 thousand folks, and about as menny more individuals; the individuals spend their time going up and down the back stairs and taking fisick. The natur ov the sile around here is sandy, and pine trees, about half and half. Thare is a rase course here, built in a sircile, whare tha make hosses go round and round; tis delitcsum tu behold! Three miles out east of the village tha hav built a fashionable pond; evrybody goes thare tu spend their munny; tha ask 8 cents a glass for their whiska! The sosietah here is permiskus, blaklegs and deakons, divines and pugerlistics, judges and jockeys, congressmen and harlots, devils and Quakers, so judciously mixed up, 'tis food for the filosopick mind. A grate menny young wimmin are brought here annually tu git married; the kourting is all did by the mothers, in fac the wimmin du it all here excep pay the bills. A man at Saratoger don't hav enny more tu sa, or du, than an old gander dus when a goose is setting. The citizens ov this place hav onla one kind ov religion or pollyticks, and that is congriss water. I kant rite enny more just now, i hav got tu go down stairs.

Aju, JOSH BILLINGS.

LXXV.

SPIRITUAL BELIEF OV THE BILLINGSES.

We beleaf in ardent spirits — sich az charitee, parsaveranse, and patrotism. We beleaf in animil spirits — sich az fast hosses, vigerous cats, and ambishus rat terriers. We beleaf in the spirits ov 76 — sich az ole Jamaka, and Santa Cruize, jist a little for the rumatiz. We beleaf in the evidence ov departed spirits, a good deal — sich az temprance houses, lemonade picknix, and water kure establishments. We beleaf in the spirits of just men — but beleaf they ar skase. We beleaf in the spirit ov revenge — if a muskeeter bites you without provocation, kill awl the muskeeters, nex ov kin, in the naberhood. We beleaf in the spirit ov forgiveness — if we owe a man, and we won't pay him, let him forgiv the det.

LXXVI.

JOSH BILLINGS CORRESPONDS WITH A "HAIR OIL AND VEGETABLE BITTERS MAN."

Dear Doktor Hirsute : — I reseaved a tin cup ov yure "Hair purswader," also a bottle ov yure Salvashum Bitters," bi express, for which, I express my thanks. The greenbak, which yu enklozed waz the kind ov purswader that we ov the press fully understand. Yur hair greese, shall hav a reglar gimnastik puff, jist az soon az i kan find a spare time. I tried a little ov it on an old counter brush in my offiss, this morning, and in 15 minnitts, the brussells grew az long az a hosses tale, and i notis this afternoon, the hair begins tew cum up thru, on bak ov the brush, 'tis really wonderful! 'tis almoste Eureka! I rubbed a drop or two on the head ov mi cane, which haz bin bald for more than 5 years, and beggar me! if I don't hav to shave the cane handle, evry day, before I can walk out with it. I hav a verry favrite cat, she iz one ov the Hambletonian breed ov cats, and altho she iz young, and haint bin trained yet, she shows grate signs ov speed. I thought I would just rob the corck ov the bottle on the floor, in the corner ov the room whare the cat generally repozes. The consequents waz, sum ov the "purswader" got onto the hair ov the cat's tale. When the cat aroze from her slumbers she caught sight ov her tale, which had growed tew an exalted size; taking one more look at the tale, she started, and bi the good olde Mozes! sich running; across the yard! over the fence! up wun side ov an apple tree! and down the other! out into the fields, away! away! The laste i saw ov the cat, she waz pretty mutch awl tale. I wouldn't hav took 10 dollars for the cat, with her old tale on her. In a fu daze, i shall find a spare time, and then i shall write up, for our paper sumthing pyroteknik, which will make the hair grow on the head ov a number 2 mackrel, to read it.

Dear Doktor, the fact iz, "sum men are born grate, sum men git grate after they are born, and sum men hav grateness hove upon them." Doctor, you are awl 3 ov these men, in one. You are a kind ov vegatable trinity, sassyfrass, pokeroot, and elderberry. It waz a happee thought in you, tew call your "Salvashun Bitters" a "vegatabel tonicks," although, old rye aint one ov the vegatabels, whiskee iz one ov the tonicks. The peopel must hev tonicks, and the more vegatabels you kan git into the gratest amount ov whiskee, the more the peopel will luv you. Thare is nothing the christian world long for so mutch, just now, as a vegatabel bitter. Sassyfrass is good for a lonesum stummuk, pokeroot is an alteratiff, and Elderberry was known to the anshients, but what! oh tell me what! yee whispring winds, what! are awl these without whiskee. Thank the Lord, that at laste, we hav got a bitter, that will tonick a man up. Nothing, sinze the good old daze ov Jamaka Rum, and sider Brandee, haz sent sich a thrill ov joy thru the wurld, az "Hirsute's Salvashun Bitters," sold respektably bi awl druggists, far and near.

Go on Doktur, manafaktring, and selling, let the cod liver, and pattent truss men, howl out in envy, let pills rant, and plasters rave, you hav got what the wurld wants, and will have, and that iz, an erb bitter, with a broad whiskee basis.

N. B. — Bizziness, Doctor, iz bizziness. The hi

prise ov material, and laber, haz put up puffs with us, but upon the reseipt ov 50 Dollars more, yu kan rely upon sumthing, in our weekly, that will send "Salvashun, and Purswashun" whirling thru the land.

P. S.— Let me advize yu az a friend; if it iz indispensible necessary tew cheat a little, in the manufakter ov the "Salvashun Bitters," let it by awl means be in the rutes, dont lower the basis.

   Yures quietly,
        JOSH BILLINGS.

LXXVII.

PROVERBS.

He who buys begrudgingly, pays the higest prise and gits nothing that sutes him.

It iz jist about az mutch mizery tew *want* a dimond ring, as tew *want* a shirt.

The author who rites for bred, wil giv hiz reeders a taste ov emptins.

I never knu a fool who hadn't a good voice.

Thieves hunt in couples, but a liar has no accomplice.

Az men gro older, their opinyuns, like their disscazes, grow kronick.

' Wimmin *luv* their hustbands, but tha *worship* their bonnets.

The man who kant liv a week on hope, and then maik a harty meal on the result is no philozopher.

I often cum akross inidividoals, quite oftenly, who think tha hav never committed enny sins or indiscreshuns in this life, such people i pitty, for they wont kno when they git to heaven.

Az a gineral thing, if yu want tew git at the truth ov a perlitikal argyment, hear both sides and beleave neither.

Thare iz a multitude of folks who mean well enuff but how like the devel tha act.

Opportunitays, like eggs don't kum but one at a time.

I luv to gaze upon a hily eddikated and intilektooal woman, but I kant sa that I want tew belong tew one ov this klass.

True honour iz a keen perception ov what iz rite, falze honour iz a keen affectashun ov what iz rong.

"Giv the devil hiz due," reads wel enuff in a proverb, but mi friend what will bekum ov you and me if this arrangement iz carried out?

If yu are happy, dont proklaim it tew the world, the world dont luv tew hear about sich things.

A jest iz sumthing that a fule admires, and a wize man laffs at.

Vartue that haint bin tempted, and wine that haint bin tasted, iz verry good vartue, and verry good wine, in bottles.

Thare iz jist this difference between a fule and a hen, the fule cackels before, and the hen not till after the egg iz lade.

LXXVIII.

DOMESTIK RECEIPTS IN FULL.

Tew sarve up cowcumbers — pick them when the dew is on them, pare them neatly, slice them thin, add salt and let them stand for 60 minnitts, pepper them freely, add good sharpe vinegar, and then — raze up the window carefully, and throw them out.

Tew make watermelons the old fashioned wa — steal them bi moonlite, and eat them in the next lot.

Lobsters want tew be boiled whole till they are ded, pour ice cream over them, send for the docktor, eat them before going tu bed, and tell yure friends the next da, that yu hav bin threatened with an attak ov the — rebbels.

Tew remove goose pimples — skin the goose.

Women's Rights Convention—Mrs. Peleg Pewter takes the chair.
—See page 200.

Tew kure hams — bathe them in Hostetter's Bitters.

Tew bring up a child in the wa he should go — travel that wa yourself.

LXXIX.

FAKS.

Josh Billings, begs leaf tu state:

That onions are *good* for a *bad* breth.

That Rockawa clams are a good opening for enny yung man.

That ships are kalled *she* bekauze tha alwus keep a man on the *lookout*.

That "turning water into wine" is a mirakle in theze days worth, at least, 300 per cent.

That boys aint ap to turn out well who dont git up till 10 o'clock in the morning.

That, if a man is agoing tu make a bizness ov sarving the Lord, he likes tu see him du it when he measures up onions as well as when he hollers glory halleluyer!

That wisdum aint nothing more than edikated cunning.

LXXX.

ON LECTURES.

Dec. 9, 1864.

I take my pen in hand, to inform you, that i am in the Lekturing bizzness. I have jined the army ov martyrs, and am having a healthy time. I lektured laste nite, tew a flooded house. Had a revival, evry fu minnits, it would hav did yu good, tew hear the people holler. The way things look now, i think i shall be able tew retire from private life, in a fu months, and keep 3 or 4 dogs, and a fish pond. Yesterday, i reseaved a dunnin letter, from mi fashionable tailor, for a coat, that has bin wore out, more than 2 years. I replied tew the limited cuss, briefly, as follers: "Dear sur — Enklozed, pleze find 20 dollars — if yu can. Yures, sum, Josh Billings.

I thought i would try a tragik lektur at fust, but tragediz are gitting so common, now a daze, that yu kan git them done, and warrented, for 25 dollars.

Mi Lektur is the normal comick, with an okasional effort tew be witty.

I hope you are well, and hav a good appetight. Remember me kindly tew Reub Fenton, when yu see him.— I also reseaved 2 letters bi to daez male, which i will let yu answer for me, thru yure valuable collums.— One ov them is from an individoal, who sines his name "Hennery," and tuther is from a person bi the name ov "Mirakle."

Hennery: — The best time tew sett a hen, is when the hen is reddy. I kant tell you what the best breed is, but the shanghigh is the meanest. It kosts as mutch tew board one, as it duz a stage hoss, and yu mite as well undertake tew fat a fanning-mill, by running oats thru it. Thare aint no proffitt in keeping a hen for his eggs, if he laze less than one a day. Hens are very long lived, if they dont contrakt the thrut disseaze,— thare is a grate menny goes tew pot, evry year, bi this melankolly disseaze. I kant tell exactly how tew pick out a good hen, but as a genral thing, the long-eared ones, are kounted the best. The one-legged ones, i kno, are the lest ap tew skratch up the garden. Eggs packed in eqnal parts ov salt, and lime water, with the other end down, will keep from 30, or 40, years, if they are not disturbed. Fresh beef-stake is good for hens; i serpoze 4 or 5 pounds a day, would be awl a hen would need, at fust along. I shall be happee tew advise with yu, at enny time, on the hen question, and — take it in egg.

Mirakle : — Yu sa " yu kant understand the mirakle ov the whale, that swallered Joner. I dont serpoze that Joner, nor the whale, ever fully understood it themselfs. I hav thought that it was eazyer for the whale tew swaller Joner, than it was for the outsiders, tew swaller the mirakel. I kant tell yu what Joner did while in the whale's sosiety ; but i kno what a yankee would hav did, he would hav rigged a rudder on the animal, and run him into port, and either klaimed the ile for salvage, or sold out his chanse tew a petroleun grease company.

LXXX.

YANKEE NOSHUNS.

The noshun that skule houzens are cheaper than stait prizens.

The noshun that men are a better krop tew raize than enny thing else.

The noshun that the whole wurld is the markit for a man's wits.

The noshun that a people who hav branes enuff kant be governed bi enny body but themselfs.

The noshun that if yu kant make a man think az yu do, try and make him do az yu think.

The noshun that the United States iz liable at any time tew be doubled, but aint liable at enny time tew be divided.

The noshun that Uncle Sam kan thrash hiz own children when tha need it, and kan thrash the hole wurld besides.

The noshun that Yankees are a fourordained rase, and kant be kept from spredding, and striking in, enny more than turpentine kan when it once gits luce.

LXXXII.

ATTENTION! SQUAD!

Men kalkulate with perfek accurasy, the rate ov speed attained bi earthly boddys, and ov moste matter, whether sublunary, or ov a heavenly natur. They tell us how long a ra ov light is on the way from the sun — how fass a comet travels — the best time that lightning can make — when the stars visit, and how long they are about it — the fraktional lapse kontained in the hop ov a flea — the flite ov a swallow — the velosity ov sound, and the smartness ov a hurrycane. They kan tell us how long it takes old Borus, after he leaves his cave, to reach this earth, and button up the coats ov shivring mortals. But i hav sarched their theorys and ransacked their mathematicks in vain, tew diskover the haste ov a Slander. But we kno ov nothing, on the earth, or above it, that equals it in quickness. It travels as well in the dark, as in the light — knows no law

Josh Billings delivers an extemporaneous political lecture.—
See page 219.

ov gravitashun, nor ov heat, or cold — is not traceable, or definable — has no parentage, and frequently no objek — is not matter, nor an essence — may fly in the glance ov an eye, or be felt in the point ov a finger — is the pet ov almost evry one — can hav the ear when charity, love, and the delikate pashuns, plead in vain — is everywhare in an instant — feeds upon nothing but sweet things, has more friends than truth, is a lie, faster than the wings ov the wind, and twin racer to thought — steals into the sakred pulpit — at midnite, robs the chaste maiden ov the ruddy truth in her cheeks — hangs sackcloth upon the manly form ov honesta — cums in a whisper — is misterious as an echo — will betray for a prise — has made kings tremble — has dried up the warm pulse ov hope, and driven modesta shrecking away — is a skorpion, invisible, but full ov madness, and menny stings. Who kan tell its whereabouts? Who can rate its speed? Who kan annylize its meanness? Who has not listened tew its preshious falsehoods? and who will not, with me, pronounse it a renegade, the common enemy ov humanitee? and who that kan shoot flieing, will not help tew bring down the base bird? Attenshun, squad!

LXXXIII.

THE FUST BABY.

The fust baby has bekum one ov the fixed stars ov life; and ever since the fust one was born, on the rong side of the gardin ov Eden, down tew the little stranger ov yesterday, they hav never failed tew be a budget ov mutch joy — an event ov mutch gladness. Tew wake up some cheerful morning, and cee a pair ov soft eyes looking into yours — to wonder how so mutch buty could have been entrusted to you — to sarch out the father, or the mother, in the sweet little fase, and then loze the survey, in an instant of buty, as a laffing Angel lays before you — tew pla with the golden hare, and sow fond kisses upon this little bird in yure nest — tiz this that makes the fust baby, the joy ov awl joys — a feast ov the harte. Tew find the pale Mother again bi yure side, more luvly than when she was wooed — tew see a new tenderness in her eye, and tew hear the chastened sweetness ov her laff, as she tells something new about 'Willie"— tew luv her far more than ever, and tew find oftimes a prayer on yure lips — tiz this that makes the fust baby a fountain ov sparkling plezzure. Tew watch the bud on yure rosebush, tew ketch the fust notes ov yure song-bird, tew hear the warm praze ov kind frends, and tew giv up yure hours tew the trezzure — tiz this that makes the fust baby a gift that Angels hav brought yu. Tew look upon the trak that life takes — tew see the sunshine and shower — tew plead for the best, and shrink from the wust — tew shudder when sikness steals on, and tew be chastened when death comes — tiz this — oh! tiz this that makes the fust baby a hope upon arth, and a gem up in heaven.

LXXXIV.

LAUGHING.

Laughing is strikly an amuzement, altho some folks make a bizzness ov it. It haz bin considered an index ov karakter, and thare iz sum, so close at reasoning, that they say, they kan tell what a man had for dinner, by seeing him laff. I never saw two laff alike. While thare are some, who dont make enny noise, thare are sum, who dont make ennything but noise; and sum agin, who hav musik in their laff, and others, who laff just az a rat duz, who haz caught a steel trap, with his tale. Thare is no mistake in the assershun, that it is a cumfert tew hear sum laffs, that cum rompin out ov a man's mouth, just like a distrik school ov yung girls, let out tew play. Then agin thare iz sum laffs, that are az kold and meaningless az a yesterday's bukwheat pancake, — that cum out ov the mouth twisted, and gritty, az a 2 inch auger, drawed out ov a hemlok board. One ov these kind ov laffs haz no more cumfert in it than the — stummuk ake haz, and makes yu feel, when yu hear it, az though yu waz being shaved bi a dull razer, without the benefit ov soap, or klergy. Men who never laff may have good hearts, but they are deep seated, — like sum springs, they hav their inlet and outlet from below, and show no sparkling bubble on the brim. I don't like a gigler, this kind ov laff iz like the dandylion, a feeble yeller, and not a bit ov good smell about it. It iz true that enny kind ov a laff iz better than none, — but giv me the laff that looks out ov a man's eyes fust, to see if the coast is clear, then steals down into the dimple ov his cheek, and rides in an eddy thare awhile, then waltzes a spell, at the korners ov his mouth, like a thing ov life, then busts its bonds ov buty, and fills the air for a moment with a shower ov silvery tongued sparks, — then steals bak, with a smile, to its lair, in the harte, tew watch agin for its prey,— this it is the kind ov laff that i luv, and aint afrade ov.

LXXXV.

PIONEERS.

God bless the pironeers — the whole ov them — inkluding the man who fust rode a mule. Hiz name waz Stickfasst, he will be remembered az long az black wax will be, hiz posterity have aul bin good stickers, sum ov the best clothes-pins the world ever saw, cum from this familee. . . . . I remember olde Buffaloo. He waz a sunsett pironeer; he started tew discover, "out west," 40 years ago, hiz property was a wife, with the side ake, 2 galls, just busting thru their clothes into womanhood, 2 boys, who kould kill a skunk at 3 paces, and dodge the smell, a one-hoss wagging, a rifle, and a brass-kittle. he squat at Rock River, in the Illinoise, for 6 months, and then moved on more westly, the last that ware seen ov him, was the hind-board ov hiz wagging, just doubling the top ov the rocky mountains. . . . . And thare waz Beltrigging, who fust diskovered the tempranse question, he had bin a suckcessful rumdrinker, and seller for 36 years, and had retired with a pile, he diskovered kold water one day, on the back side ov hiz farm, digging out foxes; he lektured nex day, in a 7-day babtiss church, and told his xperiense; he made 13 hundred dollars lekturing, and died 9 years afterwards, in grate agony, having drank 4 drops ov french brandee, on a lump ov brown sugar bi mistake. He begot Springwater, and Springwater begot Rainwater, and Rainwater begot Dewdrow, and Dewdrop begot Morning-Mist, awl ov them selebrated tempranse lekturers. . . . . And there waz Solomon Saw-dust, the author ov bran-bred, and nailrod-soup; he waz a champion ov lite weights; he fit the dispepshee in aul its forms; he lived for 18 months, at one heat, on the smell ov a red herring, and gained 9 pounds in wind. He had menny admirers and immitaturs the moste grate ov which was Wet Pack and Water Kure. . . . . And there waz Mehitable Saffron, the virgin-hero ov wimmins' rights; i herd her fust orashun, in the town hall; she spoke without notes, at arms' length. She ced, " woman had a destiny that man kouldn't fill for her, and az for her, she could go it alone, she didn't want no he-creeter around her, she had on a pair of kowhide pegged boots, and closed up bi holding hi in the air, a pair ov corduroy breeches, which she swore bi the good olde Mozes, waz awl enny man had to brag ov. . . She waz the first pironeer in the corduroy britches business, she died celibate, and haz had menny followers amung her sexes, but none that had the jism she had. . . . . And then thare waz Old Perpetual; he got crazee at last, but not till he had invented a pitch-pine dog, with a basswood tail, that would bark and chase every wagging that cum along, clean down to the bridge over bean kreek. He got out a patent for a sorrel horse, and a nu milch cow, and lived till he was 90 years olde, and then died from a kold he had caught, down seller, trieing tew make soft sope, out ov bull's liver. On hiz grave stun waz these affekting paragraph: "State, and county rights for sale, enquire ov —— the widder."

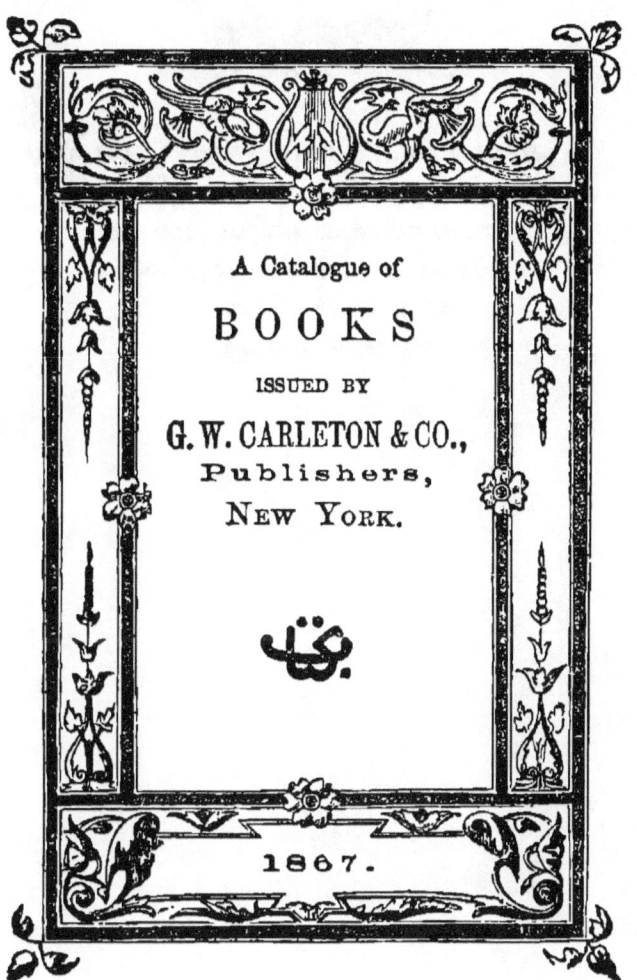

A Catalogue of

BOOKS

ISSUED BY

G. W. CARLETON & CO.,
Publishers,
NEW YORK.

بتاب

1867.

"*There is a kind of physiognomy in the titles of books no less than in the faces of men, by which a skilful observer will know as well what to expect from the one as the other.*"—BUTLER.

NEW BOOKS

And New Editions Recently Published by

G. W. CARLETON & CO.,
NEW YORK.

GEORGE W. CARLETON.   HENRY S. ALLEN.

N.B.—THE PUBLISHER, upon receipt of the price in advance, will send any of the following Books by mail, POSTAGE FREE, to any part of the United States. This convenient and very safe mode may be adopted when the neighboring Booksellers are not supplied with the desired work. State name and address in full.

Victor Hugo.

LES MISÉRABLES.—*The best edition*, two elegant 8vo. vols., beautifully bound in cloth, $5.50 ; half calf, $10.00
LES MISÉRABLES.—*The popular edition*, one large octavo volume, paper covers, $2.00 ; cloth bound, $2.50
LES MISÉRABLES.—In the Spanish language. Fine 8vo. edition, two vols., paper covers, $4.00 ; cloth bound, $5.00
JARGAL.—A new novel. Illustrated. . 12mo. cloth, $1.75
THE LIFE OF VICTOR HUGO.—By himself. 8vo. cloth, $1.75

Miss Muloch.

JOHN HALIFAX.—A novel. With illustration. 12mo. cloth, $1.75
A LIFE FOR A LIFE.— . do. do. $1.75

Charlotte Bronte (Currer Bell).

JANE EYRE.—A novel. With illustration. 12mo., cloth, $1.75
THE PROFESSOR.—do. . do. . do. $1.75
SHIRLEY.— . do. . do. . do. $1.75
VILLETTE.— . do. . do. . do. $1.75

Hand-Books of Society.

THE HABITS OF GOOD SOCIETY; with thoughts, hints, and anecdotes, concerning nice points of taste, good manners, and the art of making oneself agreeable. The most entertaining work of the kind ever published. 12mo. cloth, $1.75
THE ART OF CONVERSATION.—With directions for self-culture. A sensible and instructive work, that ought to be in the hands of every one who wishes to be either an agreeable talker or listener. . . . . 12mo. cloth, $1.50
THE ART OF AMUSING.—A collection of graceful arts, games, tricks, puzzles, and charades, intended to amuse everybody, and enable all to amuse everybody else. With suggestions for private theatricals, tableaux, parlor and family amusements, etc. With nearly 150 illustrative pictures. 12mo. cloth. $2.00

LIST OF BOOKS PUBLISHED

Mrs. Mary J. Holmes' Works.

LENA RIVERS.—	A novel.	12mo. cloth,	$1.50
DARKNESS AND DAYLIGHT.—	do.	do.	$1.50
TEMPEST AND SUNSHINE.—	do.	do.	$1.50
MARIAN GREY.—	do.	do.	$1.50
MEADOW BROOK.—	do.	do.	$1.50
ENGLISH ORPHANS.—	do.	do.	$1.50
DORA DEANE.—	do.	do.	$1.50
COUSIN MAUDE.—	do.	do.	$1.50
HOMESTEAD ON THE HILLSIDE.—	do.	do.	$1.50
HUGH WORTHINGTON.—	do.	do.	$1.50

Artemus Ward.

HIS BOOK.—The first collection of humorous writings by A. Ward. Full of comic illustrations. 12mo. cloth, $1.50

HIS TRAVELS.—A comic volume of Indian and Mormon adventures. With laughable illustrations. 12mo. cloth, $1.50

Miss Augusta J. Evans.

BEULAH.—A novel of great power.		12mo. cloth,	$1.75
MACARIA.— do. do.		do.	$1.75
ST. ELMO.— do. do.	*Just published.*	do.	$2.00

By the Author of "Rutledge."

RUTLEDGE.—A deeply interesting novel.	12mo. cloth,	$1.75
THE SUTHERLANDS.— do.	do.	$1.75
FRANK WARRINGTON.— do.	do.	$1.75
ST. PHILIP'S.— do.	do.	$1.75
LOUIE'S LAST TERM AT ST. MARY'S.	do.	$1.75
ROUNDHEARTS AND OTHER STORIES.—For children.	do.	$1.75
A ROSARY FOR LENT.—Devotional readings.	do.	$1.75

Josh Billings.

HIS BOOK.—All the rich comic sayings of this celebrated humorist. With comic illustrations. 12mo. cloth, $1.50

Mrs. Ritchie (Anna Cora Mowatt).

FAIRY FINGERS.—A capital new novel.	12mo. cloth,	$1.75
THE MUTE SINGER.— do.	do.	$1.75
A NEW BOOK.—*In press.*	do.	$1.75

New English Novels.

BEYMINSTRE.—A very interesting novel.	12mo. cloth,	$1.75
RECOMMENDED TO MERCY.— do.	do.	$1.75
TAKEN UPON TRUST.— do.	do.	$1.75

Geo. W. Carleton.

OUR ARTIST IN CUBA.—A humorous volume of travels; with fifty comic illustrations by the author. 12mo. cloth, $1.50

OUR ARTIST IN PERU.— $1.50

A. S. Roe's Works.

A LONG LOOK AHEAD.—	A novel.	12mo. cloth,	$1.50
TO LOVE AND TO BE LOVED.—	do.	do.	$1.50
TIME AND TIDE.—	do.	do.	$1.50
I'VE BEEN THINKING.—	do.	do.	$1.50
THE STAR AND THE CLOUD.—	do.	do.	$1.50
TRUE TO THE LAST.—	do.	do.	$1.50
HOW COULD HE HELP IT?—	do.	do.	$1.50
LIKE AND UNLIKE.—	do.	do.	$1.50
LOOKING AROUND.—	do.	do.	$1.50
WOMAN, OUR ANGEL.—*Just published.*		do.	$1.50

Richard B. Kimball.

WAS HE SUCCESSFUL.—	A novel.	12mo. cloth,	$1.75
UNDERCURRENTS.—	do.	do.	$1.75
SAINT LEGER.—	do.	do.	$1.75
ROMANCE OF STUDENT LIFE.—	do.	do.	$1.75
IN THE TROPICS.—	do.	do.	$1.75
THE PRINCE OF KASHNA.—	do.	do.	$1.75
EMILIE.—A sequel to "St. Leger." *In press.*		do.	$1.75

Orpheus C. Kerr.

THE ORPHEUS C. KERR PAPERS.—Comic letters and humorous military criticisms. Three series.   12mo. cloth, $1.50

Edmund Kirke.

AMONG THE PINES.—A Southern sketch.		12mo. cloth,	$1.50
MY SOUTHERN FRIENDS.—	do.	do.	$1.50
DOWN IN TENNESSEE.—	do.	do.	$1.50
ADRIFT IN DIXIE.—	do.	do.	$1.50
AMONG THE GUERILLAS.—	do.	do.	$1.50

T. S. Arthur's New Works.

LIGHT ON SHADOWED PATHS.—A novel.		12mo. cloth,	$1.50
OUT IN THE WORLD.—	do.	do.	$1.50
NOTHING BUT MONEY.—	do.	do.	$1.50
WHAT CAME AFTERWARDS.—	do.	do.	$1.50
OUR NEIGHBORS.—*Just published.*		do.	$1.50

Robinson Crusoe.

A handsome illustrated edition, complete.   12mo. cloth, $1.50

Joseph Rodman Drake.

THE CULPRIT FAY.—A faery poem.   12mo. cloth, $1.25
AN ILLUSTRATED EDITION.—With 100 exquisite illustrations on wood.   Quarto, beautifully printed and bound, $5.00

Algernon Charles Swinburne.

LAUS VENERIS—and other Poems and Ballads. 12mo. cloth. $1.75

Cuthbert Bede.
VERDANT GREEN.—A rollicking, humorous novel of English student life; with 200 comic illustrations.   12mo. cloth, $1.50

Private Miles O'Reilly.
BAKED MEATS OF THE FUNERAL.—A comic book. 12mo. cloth, $1.75
LIFE AND ADVENTURES—with comic illustrations.   do. $1.50

M. Michelet's Remarkable Works.
LOVE (L'AMOUR).—From the French. . . 12mo. cloth, $1.50
WOMAN (LA FEMME).—   do.   .   .   .   do. $1.50

J. Sheridan Le Fanu.
WYLDER'S HAND.—A powerful new novel. 12mo. cloth, $1.75
THE HOUSE BY THE CHURCHYARD.— do.   do. $1.75

Rev. John Cumming, D.D., of London.
THE GREAT TRIBULATION.—Two series.   12mo. cloth, $1.50
THE GREAT PREPARATION.—   do.   .   do. $1.50
THE GREAT CONSUMMATION.— do.   .   do. $1.50
THE LAST WARNING CRY.—   ,.   .   do. $1.50

Ernest Renan.
THE LIFE OF JESUS.—From the French work. 12mo. cloth, $1.75
THE APOSTLES.—   .   do.   .   do. $1.75

Popular Italian Novels.
DOCTOR ANTONIO.—A love story. By Ruffini. 12mo. cloth, $1.75
VINCENZO.—   do.   do.   do. $1.75
BEATRICE CENCI.—By Guerrazzi, with portrait.   do. $1.75

Charles Reade.
THE CLOISTER AND THE HEARTH.—A magnificent new novel—the best this author ever wrote.   .   .   8vo. cloth, $2.00

The Opera.
TALES FROM THE OPERAS.—A collection of clever stories, based upon the plots of all the famous operas. 12mo. cloth, $1.50

Robert B. Roosevelt.
THE GAME-FISH OF THE NORTH.—Illustrated. 12mo. cloth, $2.00
SUPERIOR FISHING.—   do.   do. $2.00
THE GAME-BIRDS OF THE NORTH.—   do. $2.00

John Phœnix.
THE SQUIBOB PAPERS.—A new humorous volume, filled with comic illustrations by the author.   12mo. cloth, $1.50

Matthew Hale Smith.
MOUNT CALVARY.—Meditations in sacred places. 12mo. $2.00

P. T. Barnum.
THE HUMBUGS OF THE WORLD.—Two series. 12mo. cloth, $1.75

BY GEO. W. CARLETON, NEW YORK.

Dr. J. J. Craven.
THE PRISON-LIFE OF JEFFERSON DAVIS.—Incidents and conversations connected with his captivity. 12mo. cloth. $2.00

Captain Raphael Semmes.
THE CRUISE OF THE ALABAMA AND SUMTER.— 12mo. cloth, $2.00

Pulpit Pungencies.
A new serio-comic religious book.—Very rich. 12mo. cl., $1.75

The Abbe Guettee.
THE PAPACY.—Its origin and schism with the Greeks. Introduction by A. Cleveland Coxe, D.D. 12mo. cloth, $1.75

Mansefield T. Walworth.
STORMCLIFF.—A new American novel. 12mo. cloth, $1.75

Amelia B. Edwards.
BALLADS.—By author of "Barbara's History." 12mo. cloth, $1.50

Mrs. Jervey (Caroline H. Glover).
HELEN COURTENAY'S PROMISE.—A new novel. 12mo. cloth, $1.75

Walter Barrett, Clerk.
THE OLD MERCHANTS OF NEW YORK.—Personal incidents, sketches, bits of biography, and events in the life of leading merchants in New York. Four series. . . . 12mo. cloth, $1.75

Madame Octavia Walton Le Vert.
SOUVENIRS OF TRAVEL. New edition. Large 12mo. cloth, $2.00

Kate Marstone.
A new and very interesting tale. . . 12mo. cloth, $1.50

By "Sentinel."
WHO GOES THERE?—Or men and events. 12mo. cloth, $1.50

Junius Brutus Booth.
MEMORIALS OF "THE ELDER BOOTH."—The actor. 12mo. cloth, $1.50

H. T. Sperry.
COUNTRY LOVE vs. CITY FLIRTATION.—A capital new society tale, with twenty superb illustrations by Hoppin. 12mo. cloth, $2.00

Epes Sargent.
PECULIAR.—A remarkable new novel. 12mo. cloth, $1.75

Cuyler Pine.
MARY BRANDEGEE.—A very powerful novel. 12mo. cloth, $1.75
A NEW NOVEL.—*In press.* . . . do. $1.75

Elisha Kent Kane.
LOVE-LIFE OF DR. KANE and Margaret Fox. 12mo. cloth, $1.75

Mother Goose for Grown Folks.
HUMOROUS RHYMES for grown people. 12mo. cloth, $1.25

Miscellaneous Works.

JOHN S. MOSBY.—His Life and Exploits, portraits. 12mo.		$1.75
THE SHENANDOAH.—History of the Conf. steamer.	do.	$1.50
TIFFITH LANK.—A travestie by W. H. Webb. *Ill.*	do.	50 cts.
NOTES ON SHAKSPEARE.—By Jas. H. Hackett. 12mo. cloth,		$1.50
THE MONTANAS.—A novel by Mrs. S. J. Hancock.	do.	$1.75
PASTIMES WITH LITTLE FRIENDS.—Martha H. Butt.	do.	$1.50
A SPINSTER'S STORY.—A new novel.	do.	$1.75
A LIFE OF JAMES STEPHENS.—Fenian Head-Centre.	do.	$1.00
FREE GOVERNMENT IN ENGLAND AND AMERICA.—	do.	$3.00
AUTOBIOGRAPHY OF A NEW ENGLAND FARM-HOUSE.—	do.	$1.75
NEPENTHE.—A new novel.	do.	$1.50
TOGETHER.— do.	do.	$1.50
LOVERS AND THINKERS.—do.	do.	$1.50
POEMS.—By Gay H. Naramore.	do.	$1.50
GOMERY OF MONTGOMERY.—By C. A. Washburn.	do.	$2.00
VICTOIRE.—A new novel.	do.	$1.75
POEMS.—By Mrs. Sarah T. Bolton.	do.	$1.50
SUPPRESSED BOOK ABOUT SLAVERY.—	do.	$2.00
JOHN GUILDERSTRING'S SIN.—A novel.	do.	$1.50
CENTEOLA.—By author "Green Mountain Boys."	do.	$1.50
RED TAPE AND PIGEON-HOLE GENERALS.—	do.	$1.50
TREATISE ON DEAFNESS.—By Dr. E. B. Lighthill.	do.	$1.50
AROUND THE PYRAMIDS.—By Gen. Aaron Ward.	do.	$1.50
CHINA AND THE CHINESE.—By W. L. G. Smith.	do.	$1.50
THE YACHTMAN'S PRIMER.—By T. R. Warren.	do.	50 cts.
EDGAR POE AND HIS CRITICS.—By Mrs. Whitman.	do.	$1.00
MARRIED OFF.—Illustrated Satirical Poem.	do.	50 cts.
THE FLYING DUTCHMAN.—J. G. Saxe, illustrated.	do.	75 cts.
ALEXANDER VON HUMBOLDT.—Life and Travels.	do.	$1.50
LIFE OF HUGH MILLER.—The celebrated geologist.	do.	$1.50
THE RUSSIAN BALL.—Illustrated satirical poem.	do.	50 cts.
THE SNOBLACE BALL. do. do. do.	do.	50 cts.
AN ANSWER TO HUGH MILLER.—By T. A. Davies.	do.	$1.50
COSMOGONY.—By Thomas A. Davies.	8vo. cloth	$2.00
TWENTY YEARS around the world. J. Guy Vassar.	do.	$3.75
RURAL ARCHITECTURE.—By M. Field, illustrated.	do.	$2.00

www.ingramcontent.com/pod-product-compliance
Lightning Source LLC
Chambersburg PA
CBHW021344230426

43666CB00006B/404